Our selection of the city's best places to
eat, drink and experience

◉ **Sights**

✖ **Eating**

🍷 **Drinking**

⭐ **Entertainment**

🔒 **Shopping**

...des
...e city.
...side you'll find all the
must-see sights, plus tips to
make your visit to each one
really memorable. We've split
the city into easy-to-navigate
neighbourhoods and provided
clear maps so you'll find your
way around with ease. Our
expert author has searched
out the best of the city: walks,
food, nightlife and shopping,
to name a few. Because you
want to explore, our 'Local Life'
pages will take you to some
of the most exciting areas to
experience the real Madrid.

And of course you'll find all
the practical tips you need for
a smooth trip: itineraries for
short visits: how to get around,
and how much to tip the guy
who serves you a drink at the
end of a long day's exploration.

It's your guarantee of a
really great experience.

**These symbols give you the vital
information for each listing:**

☎ Telephone Numbers	♥ Family-Friendly
◷ Opening Hours	☺ Pet-Friendly
Ⓟ Parking	☒ Bus
⊖ Nonsmoking	☒ Ferry
@ Internet Access	Ⓜ Metro
🛜 Wi-Fi Access	Ⓢ Subway
🥗 Vegetarian Selection	☒ Tram
📖 English-Language Menu	☒ Train

**Find each listing quickly on maps
for each neighbourhood:**

Bar Hemingway

16   Map p233, B2

Legend has it that Hemi
self, wielding a machine
...rate this timber-pan
...ered bar during
...showpiece is a
...en by Papa ar
... town. Dress
...s.com; Hôtel Rit
... ◷6.30pm-2a

6 ◉ Plac
Vc

Our Promise

You can trust our travel information because Lonely Planet
authors visit the places we
write about, each and every
edition. We never accept
freebies for positive coverage,
so you can rely on us to tell it
like it is.

QuickStart Guide

Welcome to Madrid

No city on earth is more alive than Madrid, a beguiling place whose sheer energy carries a simple message: this is one city that knows how to live. Madrid's calling cards are many: astonishing art galleries, stunning architecture, relentless nightlife, fine restaurants and tapas bars. Other cities have some of these things. Madrid has them all in bucketloads.

Gran Vía (p124)
KASTO80/GETTY IMAGES ©

Madrid
Top Sights

Museo del Prado (p66)

Spain's premier art gallery is also one of Europe's finest, an extraordinary collection that ranges from Goya and Velázquez to Rembrandt, Rubens and Bosch. If you visit one Madrid art gallery, make it the Museo del Prado.

Centro de Arte Reina Sofía (p72)

Where the Prado gathers together the old masters, the Reina Sofía is all about contemporary art, with Picasso, Dalí and Miró leading the way. Picasso's *Guernica* alone is worth the admission price 10 times over.

Museo Thyssen-Bornemisza (p76)

The third pillar of Madrid's triumvirate of stellar art museums, the Thyssen boasts a private collection that offers a staggering journey through the best in European art. There's scarcely a European master that doesn't make an appearance here.

Parque del Buen Retiro (p80)

This glorious and expansive parkland was once a royal hideaway, but it's now one of our favourite places in Madrid to picnic and wander amid the abundant greenery, water and beautiful monuments.

Plaza Mayor (p24)

In this city of pretty public squares, the Plaza Mayor is easily the most picturesque, combining stately architecture, a compelling history and the rich canvas of modern Madrid life.

Ermita de San Antonio de la Florida (p114)

Tucked away from Madrid's tourist heartland, this tiny hermitage contains a magnificent secret: vivid frescoes adorning the domes just as Goya painted them more than two centuries ago.

Palacio Real (p26)

Madrid's royal palace provides the backdrop to some of the city's loveliest urban views, and the interior is a lavish study in Spanish royal extravagance down through the centuries.

Plaza de Toros & Museo Taurino (p98)

Spain's spiritual home of bullfighting hosts *corridas* (bullfights) from May to October, but is always worth visiting for Moorish architecture, the fascinating museum and guided tours that take you inside this peculiarly Spanish passion.

Museo Lázaro Galdiano (p86)

One of numerous elegant mansions in the upmarket neighbourhood of Salamanca, this fine stately home contains one of Madrid's most eclectic collections of curios mixed in with artworks of the highest calibre.

San Lorenzo de El Escorial (p118)

Away in the cool mountain foothills northwest of Madrid, this palace-monastery complex is a monument to the aspirations to greatness of many a Spanish king. It's also one of Madrid's most rewarding day trips.

Madrid Local Life

Insider tips to help you find the real city

If you're looking for the perfect complement to Madrid's major sights, we introduce you to five routes through the city's neighbourhoods that show you how to experience Madrid like a local.

El Rastro Sunday (p40)

▶ Shopping
▶ Tapas and vermouth

Visiting the Sunday morning flea market of El Rastro is a Madrid institution. It tumbles down the hill from La Latina to Lavapiés, and, this being Madrid, it's always followed by a tapas-and-vermouth crawl through the bars of La Latina.

A Night Out in Huertas (p52)

▶ Classy bars, classic bars
▶ Great live music

Huertas is the city's true hub of after-dark action. Gorgeous Plaza de Santa Ana is the focal point around which so much

of the energy swirls, but the surrounding streets are filled with old bars that haven't changed in decades, rooftop bars for urban sophisticates, fabulous live-music venues and outstanding nightclubs.

Shopping in Upmarket Salamanca (p88)

▶ High fashion
▶ Gourmet food

Salamanca is the epicentre of Spain's world-renowned fashion industry. Calle de Serrano and surrounds are where the locals shop in the boutiques of Spanish designers, while the elite track down the most prestigious international

labels. Gourmet food shops and tapas bars where food is art fit perfectly in these stylish surrounds.

Counterculture in Malasaña (p102)

▶ An alternative slant
▶ Vintage Madrid

Salamanca's alter ego, down-and-dirty Malasaña is where heady 1980s Madrid still lives and breathes. It's all about retro fashions, fine old cafes and nightlife where dressing down is the done thing, and about street cred and a local clientele that effortlessly spans the spectrum from ageing *rockeros* to Madrid's cool young things.

Above: Plaza de Santa Ana, Huertas; below: El Rastro

Barrio Life in Chamberí (p116)

▶ Traditional and authentic
▶ Classic shops and bars

To understand what makes Madrid tick, spend a few hours in Chamberí just north of the centre. With intriguing sights to anchor your visit, authenticity is otherwise the key with fine old shops, classic *barrio* bars and the Plaza de Olavide, one of our favourite little squares in the city.

DAN MOORE/GETTY IMAGES ©

Other great places to experience the city like a local:

La Ideal (p34)

El Café de la Opera (p36)

Bar Santurce (p47)

Bar Melo's (p48)

La Mallorquina (p60)

Calle de la Paz (p62)

Mercado de la Paz (p92)

Calle de Pez (p112)

Bon Vivant & Co (p108)

Madrid Day Planner

Day One

So many Madrid days begin in the **Plaza Mayor** (p24), or perhaps nearby with a breakfast of *chocolate con churros* at **Chocolatería de San Ginés** (p126). While you're in the old town, drop by the **Plaza de la Villa** (p30) and **Plaza de Oriente** (p30).

Stop for a coffee or wine at **Cafe de Oriente** (p34), visit the **Palacio Real** (p26), then graze on tapas for lunch at the **Mercado de San Miguel** (p32). If you've only time to visit one Madrid art gallery, make it the peerless **Museo del Prado** (p66), where you could easily spend an entire afternoon. Wander down the Paseo del Prado to admire **Caixa Forum** (p83), before climbing up through the narrow lanes of Huertas to a pre-dinner tipple at **La Venencia** (p59).

Dinner at **Restaurante Sobrino de Botín** (p32) is a fine way to spend your evening and an experience you'll always remember. Perhaps take in a flamenco show at **Las Tablas** (p35), followed by a cocktail at **Museo Chicote** (p108). If you're up for a long night, **Teatro Joy Eslava** (p35) is an icon of the Madrid night.

Day Two

Get to the **Centro de Arte Reina Sofía** (p72) early to beat the crowds, then, after the clamour of yesterday, climb up through sedate streets to spend a couple of hours soaking up the calm of the **Parque del Buen Retiro** (p137).

Wander down to admire the **Plaza de la Cibeles** (p83), have another tapas lunch at **Estado Puro** (p124) or **Los Gatos** (p58), then catch the Metro across town to admire the Goya frescoes in the **Ermita de San Antonio de la Florida** (p114). Back in town, shop for souvenirs at **Casa de Diego** (p63), **El Arco Artesanía** (p36) and **Antigua Casa Talavera** (p36) before heading to **Café del Real** (p34) for a drink. Then it's on to Plaza de Santa Ana for another drink, or three, at an outdoor table if the weather is fine.

Check out if there's live jazz on offer at wonderful **Café Central** (p62), then have an after-show drink at **El Imperfecto** (p60) and dinner at **Vi Cool** (p57) or **Casa Alberto** (p57), depending on your mood. The night is still young – **Kapital** (p83) is good if you're in the mood to dance, **La Terraza del Urban** (p60) if you're in need of more sybaritic pleasures.

Short on time?

We've arranged Madrid's must-sees into these day-by-day itineraries to make sure you see the very best of the city in the time you have available.

Day Three

☼ Spend the morning at the third of Madrid's world-class art galleries, the **Museo Thyssen-Bornemisza** (p76), then head out east to take a tour of the **Plaza de Toros** (p98) bullring, before spending the rest of the morning shopping along Calle de Serrano.

☼ If you're feeling extravagant, try the thrilling experience of **Platea** (p95); if you've fallen in love with the idea of tapas, lunch instead at **Biotza** (p94) or **La Colonial de Goya** (p94). After lunch, spend an hour or two at the **Museo Lázaro Galdiano** (p86), before dropping down the hill for a coffee at the storied **Café-Restaurante El Espejo** (p110).

☾ As dusk approaches, catch the metro across town to La Latina and spend as long as you can picking your way through the tapas bars of Calle de la Cava Baja. A wine at **Taberna Tempranillo** (p48) and a mojito out on Plaza de la Paja at **Delic** (p41) should set you up for the night ahead. Live music is a great way to spend it, either at **Sala El Sol** (p62) or **Costello Café & Niteclub** (p63). Then lose all sense of decorum dancing the night away at **Why Not?** (p111) in Chueca.

Day Four

☼ If you really love your art, an hour or two in the morning at **Real Academia de Bellas Artes de San Fernando** (p55) will nicely round out your experience of Madrid's exceptional art scene. You've been around almost long enough to be a local, and it's therefore worth exploring the laneways of Malasaña between Calle Pez, Plaza Dos de Mayo and the Glorieta de Bilbao – stop off at **La Mucca de Pez** (p107), **Lolina Vintage Café** (p103) and **Café Manuela** (p110).

☼ Lunch at **Albur** (p108) or **Bazaar** (p106). If you've left a minimum of three hours to play with, take a train out of town to **San Lorenzo de El Escorial** (p119) to enjoy the clear mountain air and lavish palace-monastery complex.

☾ Back in town, if you've timed your run well, there's time for one last performance, this time *zarzuela* (mix of theatre, music and dance) at **Teatro de la Zarzuela** (p62). Your last night deserves a special meal – try **La Terraza del Casino** (p58) to really be blown away, although you'll need to have booked well in advance. To round out your visit, hit **Almonte** (p95) or **El Junco Jazz Club** (p112), depending on what sort of memories you'd like to leave Madrid with.

Need to Know

**For more information,
see Survival Guide (p145)**

Currency
Euros (€)

Language
Spanish (Castellano)

Visas
Generally not required for stays of up to
90 days every six months (not at all for
members of EU or Schengen countries).
Some nationalities need a Schengen visa.

Money
ATMs widely available. Credit cards widely
accepted.

Mobile Phones
Local SIM cards widely available and can
be used in European and Australian mobile
phones. Other phones may need to be set
to roaming.

Time
Western European (GMT/UTC plus one
hour during winter, plus two hours during
daylight-saving period).

Plugs & Adaptors
Plugs have two round pins;
electrical current is 220V/50Hz.

Tipping
Small change (€1 per person in restaurants)
and rounding up (in taxis) is usually sufficient.

➊ Before You Go

Your Daily Budget

Budget less than €80

▶ Dorm beds €18–€28; *hostal* (budget
hotel) doubles €55–€70

▶ Three-course *menú del día* lunches

▶ Plan sightseeing around 'free admission'
times

Midrange €80–€200

▶ Double room in midrange hotel €75–€150

▶ Lunch and/or dinner in decent restaurants

▶ Use discount cards to keep costs down

Top End more than €200

▶ Double room in top-end hotel from €150

▶ Fine dining for lunch and dinner

Useful Websites

▶ **EsMadrid.com** (www.esmadrid.com)
Tourist office's website.

▶ **LeCool** (madrid.lecool.com) Alternative,
offbeat and avant-garde.

▶ **Lonely Planet** (www.lonelyplanet.com/
madrid) An overview of Madrid with hundreds
of useful links.

▶ **Turismo Madrid** (www.turismomadrid.
es) Regional Comunidad de Madrid tourist
office site.

Advance Planning

Three months Reserve your hotel as early
as you can.

One month Book a table at DiverXo (www.
diverxo.com), La Terraza del Casino (www.
casinodemadrid.es) or Viridiana (www.
restauranteviridiana.com).

One week Book online entry to the Museo
del Prado (www.museodelprado.es) to
avoid queues on arrival.

② Arriving in Madrid

Most visitors arrive at Aeropuerto de Barajas, 12km northeast of the city. There are four terminals: T4 is separated from the others, but connected by bus and metro. Train travellers will arrive at either Chamartín or Atocha stations.

✈ From Aeropuerto de Barajas

Destination	Best Transport
Plaza Mayor & Royal Madrid	EMT Airport Bus & metro (line 2)
La Latina & Lavapiés	EMT Airport Bus & metro (line 2)
Sol, Santa Ana & Huertas	EMT Airport Bus & metro (line 2)
El Retiro & the Art Museums	EMT Airport Bus
Salamanca	Metro (lines 4, 8 & 10)
Malasaña & Chueca	Metro (lines 8 & 10)

🚆 From Estación de Atocha

Destination	Best Transport
Plaza Mayor & Royal Madrid	Metro (line 1)
La Latina & Lavapiés	Metro (lines 1 & 5)
Sol, Santa Ana & Huertas	Metro (line 1)
El Retiro & the Art Museums	Walk
Salamanca	Metro (lines 1 & 4)
Malasaña & Chueca	Metro (lines 1 & 5)

🚆 From Estación de Chamartín

This station lies north of the city centre and lines 1 and 10 connect it with the rest of Madrid. Only La Latina and Lavapiés (line 5), El Retiro and the Art Museums (line 2) and Salamanca (line 4) require a change of line.

③ Getting Around

Madrid has an efficient and comprehensive public transport system. Easily the best way to get around town is by the metro, an excellent underground rail network that covers the whole city. The bus system is also outstanding. Conveniently, both operate under the same ticketing system; it works out cheaper to purchase the 10-trip Metrobus ticket (€12.20) than individual tickets.

Ⓜ Metro

Twelve colour-coded metro lines (www.metromadrid.es) criss-cross central Madrid, although only numbers 1 to 10 are likely to be of use to travellers. All Madrid neighbourhoods have convenient stations, and the only place you're likely to need to walk any distance (and it's a lovely walk!) is along Paseo del Prado, which has metro stations at either end.

🚌 Bus

Madrid's EMT bus network nicely complements the metro and lets you see the city as you travel around. Visit www.emtmadrid.es for route maps and numbers.

🚆 Cercanías Trains

The short-range *cercanías* regional trains operated by **Renfe** (www.renfe.com/viajeros/cercanias/madrid/index.html) go as far afield as El Escorial, and they can be handy for making a quick, north–south hop between Chamartín and Atocha train stations (with stops at Nuevos Ministerios and Sol).

Madrid Neighbourhoods

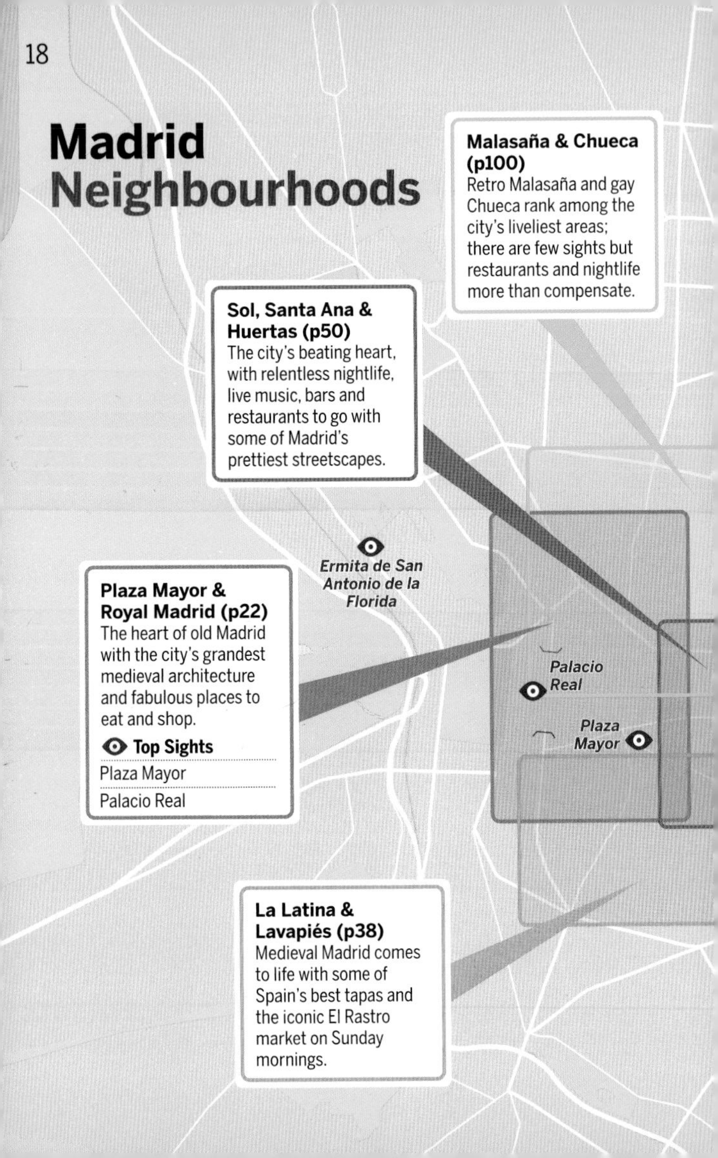

Malasaña & Chueca (p100)
Retro Malasaña and gay Chueca rank among the city's liveliest areas; there are few sights but restaurants and nightlife more than compensate.

Sol, Santa Ana & Huertas (p50)
The city's beating heart, with relentless nightlife, live music, bars and restaurants to go with some of Madrid's prettiest streetscapes.

◉ *Ermita de San Antonio de la Florida*

Plaza Mayor & Royal Madrid (p22)
The heart of old Madrid with the city's grandest medieval architecture and fabulous places to eat and shop.

◉ **Top Sights**

Plaza Mayor

Palacio Real

◉ *Palacio Real*

◉ *Plaza Mayor*

La Latina & Lavapiés (p38)
Medieval Madrid comes to life with some of Spain's best tapas and the iconic El Rastro market on Sunday mornings.

Worth a Trip

⊙ **Top Sights**

Plaza de Toros &
Museo Taurino

Ermita de San Antonio
de la Florida

San Lorenzo de
El Escorial

⊙
*Museo
Lázaro
Galdiano*

⊙
*Plaza de Toros &
Museo Taurino*

Salamanca (p84)
Upmarket, quiet
neighbourhood; fine
boutiques, designer
tapas bars and trendy
food stores make this
Madrid's home of style.

⊙ **Top Sights**
Museo Lázaro Galdiano

⊙
*Museo
Thyssen-
Bornemisza*

⊙
*Parque
del Buen
Retiro*

⊙
*Museo del
Prado*

⊙
*Centro de Arte
Reina Sofía*

**El Retiro & the Art
Museums (p64)**
Spain's golden mile of
art with a glorious park
thrown in.

⊙ **Top Sights**
Museo del Prado

Centro de Arte
Reina Sofía

Museo Thyssen-
Bornemisza

Parque del Buen Retiro

Explore
Madrid

Worth a Trip

Mercado de San Miguel (p32)
SYLVAIN SONNET/CORBIS ©

Explore

Plaza Mayor & Royal Madrid

From the heart of old Madrid to the city's historical seat of royal power, here is Madrid's story at its most grand. This is where the city's tale began and a palpable sense of history survives in the tangled laneways that open onto elegant squares, all watched over by monasteries, churches and the grand public buildings that define old Spain.

The Sights in a Day

☀ Begin with breakfast on **Plaza de Oriente** (p30) at **Cafe de Oriente** (p34), then beat the crowds by visiting the **Palacio Real** (p26) when it opens. Pause at the **cathedral** (p30), then climb Calle Mayor to intimate **Plaza de la Villa** (p30), home to distinctive Madrid architecture. Lunch at the **Mercado de San Miguel** (p32).

☀ Linger for as long you can in **Plaza Mayor** (p24), perhaps browsing the high-quality souvenirs at **El Arco Artesanía** (p36) before wandering down to the **Convento de las Descalzas Reales** (p30), one of Madrid's most extravagant interiors. Pass by **Iglesia de San Ginés** (p31), followed by a lazy afternoon mojito at **Café del Real** (p34); if you can get one of the upstairs tables by the window, you'll stay longer than planned.

☾ A busy night begins with flamenco at **Café de Chinitas** (p35) or **Las Tablas** (p35), followed by a meal at **Restaurante Sobrino de Botín** (p32). **Anticafé** (p35) is good for first drinks, followed by all-night dancing at **Teatro Joy Eslava** (p35). Just around the corner, stop for *chocolate con churros* at **Chocolatería de San Ginés** (p34) on the way home.

👁 Top Sights

Plaza Mayor (p24)

Palacio Real (p26)

♥ Best of Plaza Mayor & Royal Madrid

Eating

Mercado de San Miguel (p32)

Restaurante Sobrino de Botín (p32)

Casa Revuelta (p32)

Taberna La Bola (p32)

Architecture

Plaza Mayor (p24)

Palacio Real (p26)

Plaza de la Villa (p30)

Convento de las Descalzas Reales (p30)

Live Music

Café de Chinitas (p35)

Las Tablas (p35)

Getting There

Ⓜ **Metro** Sol is the most convenient station with lines 1, 2 and 3 all passing through. Ópera (lines 2 and 5) is right in the heart of the neighbourhood.

Ⓜ **Metro** Other stations around the periphery include Plaza de España (lines 3 and 10), Callao (1, 3 and 5) and La Latina (5).

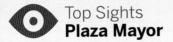

Top Sights
Plaza Mayor

It's easy to fall in love with Madrid in the Plaza Mayor. This is the monumental heart of the city and the grand stage for so many of the city's most important historical events. Here, Madrid's relentless energy courses across its cobblestones beneath ochre-hued apartments, wrought-iron balconies, frescoes and stately spires. This juxtaposition of endlessly moving city life and more static architectural attractions is Madrid in a nutshell.

👁 Map p28, D6

Plaza Mayor

Ⓜ Sol

Don't Miss

History's Tale
Designed in 1619 by Juan Gómez de Mora and built in typical Herrerian style, of which the slate spires are the most obvious expression, Plaza Mayor's first public ceremony was the beatification of San Isidro Labrador (St Isidro the Farm Labourer), Madrid's patron saint. Bullfights, often in celebration of royal weddings or births, with royalty watching on from the balconies and up to 50,000 people crammed into the plaza, were a recurring theme until 1878. Far more notorious were the *autos-da-fé* (the ritual condemnations of heretics during the Spanish Inquisition) followed by executions – burnings at the stake and deaths by garrotte on the north side of the square, hangings to the south.

Real Casa de la Panadería
The warm colours of the apartments with their 237 wrought-iron balconies are offset by the exquisite frescoes of the 17th-century **Real Casa de la Panadería** (Royal Bakery). The present frescoes date to just 1992 and are the work of artist Carlos Franco, who chose images from the signs of the zodiac and gods (eg Cybele) to provide a stunning backdrop for the plaza. The frescoes were inaugurated to coincide with Madrid's 1992 spell as European Capital of Culture.

Felipe III
In the middle of the square stands an equestrian statue of the man who ordered the plaza's construction: Felipe III. Originally placed in the Casa de Campo, it was moved to Plaza Mayor in 1848, whereafter it became a favoured meeting place for irreverent *madrileños*, who arranged to catch up 'under the balls of the horse'.

☑ Top Tips

▶ To see the plaza's epic history told in pictures, check out the carvings on the circular seats beneath the lamp posts.

▶ On Sunday mornings the plaza's arcaded perimeter is taken over by traders of old coins, banknotes and stamps.

▶ In December and early January the plaza is occupied by a Christmas market selling the season's kitsch.

▶ The bars and restaurants with outdoor tables spilling onto the plaza are often overpriced and best avoided.

✕ Take a Break

Just beyond the square's western perimeter, the Mercado de San Miguel (p32) combines historic architecture with one of Madrid's most exciting eating experiences.

For fast food Madrid style, drop down off the plaza's southeastern corner for a *bocadillo de calamares* (a roll filled with deep-fried calamari) at Bar La Ideal (p34).

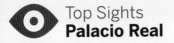

Top Sights
Palacio Real

You can almost imagine how the eyes of Felipe V, the first of the Bourbon kings, lit up when the *alcázar* (Muslim-era fortress) burned down in 1734 on Madrid's most exclusive patch of real estate. His plan? Build a palace that would dwarf all its European counterparts. The resulting 2800-room royal palace never quite attained such a scale, but it's still an Italianate baroque architectural landmark of arresting beauty, an intriguing mix of the extravagant and restrained but unmistakably elegant.

👁 Map p28, A6

www.patrimonionacional.es

Calle de Bailén

adult/concession €11/6, guide/audioguide €4/4, EU citizens free last two hours Mon-Thu

🕐 10am-8pm

Ⓜ Ópera

Don't Miss

Farmacia Real

The Farmacia Real (Royal Pharmacy), the first set of rooms to the right at the southern end of the Plaza de la Armería (Plaza de Armas; Plaza of the Armoury) courtyard, contains a formidable collection of medicine jars and stills for mixing royal concoctions; the royals were either paranoid or decidedly sickly. At the time of writing, there were plans to move the Farmacia – ask at the ticket office.

Salón del Trono

From the northern end of the Plaza de la Armería, the main stairway, a grand statement of imperial power, leads to the royal apartments and eventually to the Salón del Trono (Throne Room). The room is nauseatingly lavish with its crimson-velvet wall coverings complemented by a ceiling painted by the dramatic Venetian baroque master, Tiepolo, who was a favourite of Carlos III.

Gasparini & Porcelana

Close to the Throne Room, the Salón de Gasparini (Gasparini Room) has an exquisite stucco ceiling and walls resplendent with embroidered silks. The aesthetic may be different in the Sala de Porcelana (Porcelain Room), but the aura of extravagance continues with myriad pieces from the one-time Retiro porcelain factory screwed into the walls.

Jardines de Sabatini

The French-inspired **Jardines de Sabatini** (⏱9am-10pm May-Sep, 9am-9pm Oct-Apr; Ⓜ Ópera) lie along the northern flank of the Palacio Real. They were laid out in the 1930s to replace the royal stables that once stood on the site.

☑ Top Tips

▶ Plan to get here at 10am before the tour buses start to arrive.

▶ A colourful changing of the guard in full parade dress takes place at noon on the first Wednesday of every month (except August and September) between the palace and the cathedral.

▶ A guided tour or audioguide will greatly enhance your experience of the palace.

▶ Don't be surprised if the palace is closed for visitors because an official reception is taking place.

✗ Take a Break

There are few more beautiful vantage points than the outdoor tables at Cafe de Oriente (p34) – perfect for a coffee or wine.

Coffee, cakes and *copas* (spirits) are a winning combination at Cafe del Real (p34), just beyond the Teatro Real east of the palace.

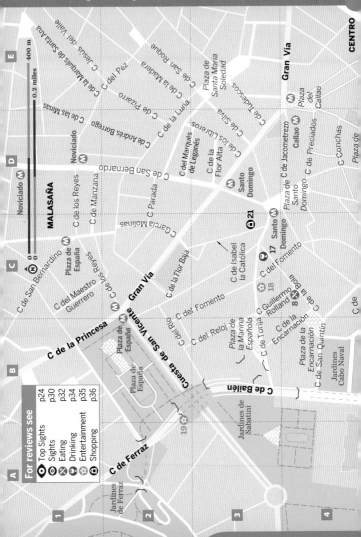

CENTRO

Gran Vía

Plaza del Callao

C de Preciados

C de Conchas

Plaza de

Plaza de Jacometrezo

Callao Ⓜ

Santo Domingo

Plaza de Santo Domingo

Gran Vía

C de Tudescos

Plaza de Santa María Soledad

C de Silva

C de los Libreros

C de la Flor Alta

C de la Luna

C del Marqués de Leganés

Santo Domingo Ⓜ

⊟ 21

C del Fomento

⊙ 17

✿ 18

C de Isabel la Católica

C de la Flor Baja

Santo Domingo Ⓜ

C Guillermo Rolland

C de la Bola

✚ 8

C de la Encarnación

Plaza de la Encarnación

C de San Quintín

C de

Jardines Cabo Naval

C de la Madera

C de San Roque

C del Pez

C de Pizarro

C de la Marqués de Santa Ana

C de Jesús del Valle

400 m

0.2 miles

C de las Minas

C de Andrés Borrego

Noviciado Ⓜ

MALASAÑA

C de San Bernardino

Plaza de España Ⓜ

C del Maestro Guerrero

C de la Princesa

C de los Reyes

C de Manzana

Noviciado Ⓜ

C de San Bernardo

C de Parada

García Molinas

Gran Vía

Plaza de España Ⓜ

Cuesta de San Vicente

C del Río

C del Fomento

C del Reloj

Plaza de la Marina Española

C de Toríja

C de Bailén

Plaza de España

Jardines de Sabatini

✿ 19

C de Ferraz

Jardines de Ferraz

Sights

Plaza de la Villa
SQUARE

1 Map p28, C6

The intimate Plaza de la Villa is one of Madrid's prettiest. Enclosed on three sides by wonderfully preserved examples of 17th-century *barroco madrileño* (Madrid-style baroque architecture – a pleasing amalgam of brick, exposed stone and wrought iron), it was the permanent seat of Madrid's city government from the Middle Ages until recent years, when Madrid's city council relocated to the grand Palacio de Cibeles on Plaza de la Cibeles (p83). (Plaza de la Villa; Ⓜ Ópera)

Convento de las Descalzas Reales
CONVENT

2 Map p28, D5

The grim plateresque walls of the Convento de las Descalzas Reales

---

☑ Top Tip

Cathedral Extras

Climb up through the Museo de la Catedral y Cúpola of the Catedral de Nuestra Señora de la Almudena on the northern facade, opposite the Palacio Real, for fine views from the top. Down the hill beneath the cathedral's southern wall on Calle Mayor is a neo-Romanesque crypt, with more than 400 columns, 20 chapels and fine stained-glass windows.

---

offer no hint that behind the facade lies a sumptuous stronghold of the faith. The compulsory guided tour (in Spanish) leads you up a gaudily frescoed Renaissance stairway to the upper level of the cloister. The vault was painted by Claudio Coello, one of the most important artists of the Madrid School of the 17th century and whose works adorn San Lorenzo de El Escorial. (Convent of the Barefoot Royals; www.patrimonionacional.es; Plaza de las Descalzas 3; admission €6, incl Real Monasterio de la Encarnación €8, EU citizens free Wed & Thu afternoon; ⊙ 10am-2pm & 4-6.30pm Tue-Sat, 10am-3pm Sun; Ⓜ Ópera, Sol)

Plaza de Oriente
SQUARE

3 Map p28, B5

A royal palace that once had aspirations to be the Spanish Versailles. Sophisticated cafes watched over by apartments that cost the equivalent of a royal salary. The Teatro Real (p36), Madrid's opera house and one of Spain's temples to high culture. Some of the finest sunset views in Madrid... Welcome to Plaza de Oriente, a living, breathing monument to imperial Madrid. (Plaza de Oriente; Ⓜ Ópera)

Catedral de Nuestra Señora de la Almudena
CATHEDRAL

4 Map p28, A6

Paris has Notre Dame and Rome has St Peter's Basilica. In fact, almost every European city of stature has

Catedral de Nuestra Señora de la Almudena

its signature cathedral, a stand-out monument to a glorious Christian past. Not Madrid. Although the exterior of the Catedral de Nuestra Señora de la Almudena sits in harmony with the adjacent Palacio Real, Madrid's cathedral is cavernous and largely charmless within; its colourful, modern ceilings do little to make up for the lack of old-world gravitas that so distinguishes great cathedrals. (☏ 91 542 22 00; www.museo catedral.archimadrid.es; Calle de Bailén; cathedral & crypt by donation, museum adult/child €6/4; ⏰ 9am-8.30pm Mon-Sat, for Mass Sun, museum 10am-2.30pm Mon-Sat; Ⓜ Ópera)

Iglesia de San Ginés   CHURCH

5 ◉ Map p28, D5

Due north of Plaza Mayor, San Ginés is one of Madrid's oldest churches: it has been here in one form or another since at least the 14th century. What you see today was built in 1645 but largely reconstructed after a fire in 1824. The church houses some fine paintings, including El Greco's *Expulsion of the Moneychangers from the Temple* (1614), which is beautifully displayed; the glass is just 6mm from the canvas to avoid reflections. (Calle del Arenal 13; ⏰ 8.45am-1pm & 6-9pm Mon-Sat, 9.45am-2pm & 6-9pm Sun; Ⓜ Sol, Ópera)

Eating

Casa Revuelta
TAPAS €

6 Map p28, D7

Casa Revuelta puts out some of Madrid's finest tapas of *bacalao* (cod) bar none – unlike elsewhere, *tajadas de bacalao* (lightly crumbed and fried cod) here don't have bones in them and slide down the throat with the greatest of ease. Early on a Sunday afternoon, as the Rastro crowd gathers here, it's filled to the rafters. ([📞]91 366 33 32; Calle de Latoneros 3; tapas from €2.80; [🕐]10.30am-4pm & 7-11pm Tue-Sat, 10.30am-4pm Sun, closed Aug; [M]Sol, La Latina)

Mercado de San Miguel
TAPAS €€

7 Map p28, C6

One of Madrid's oldest and most beautiful markets, the Mercado de San Miguel has undergone a stunning major renovation. Within the early-20th-century glass walls, the market has become an inviting space strewn with tables. You can order tapas and sometimes more substantial plates at most of the counter-bars, and everything here (from caviar to chocolate)

is as tempting as the market is alive. (www.mercadodesanmiguel.es; Plaza de San Miguel; tapas from €1; [🕐]10am-midnight Sun-Wed, 10am-2am Thu-Sat; [M]Sol)

Taberna La Bola
MADRILEÑO €€

8 Map p28, C4

Taberna La Bola (going strong since 1870 and run by the sixth generation of the Verdasco family) is a much-loved bastion of traditional Madrid cuisine. If you're going to try *cocido a la madrileña* (meat-and-chickpea stew; €21) while in Madrid, this is a good place to do so. ([📞]91 547 69 30; www.labola.es; Calle de la Bola 5; mains €16-24; [🕐]1.30-4.30pm & 8.30-11pm Mon-Sat, 1.30-4.30pm Sun, closed Aug; [M]Santo Domingo)

Casa María
SPANISH €€

9 Map p28, D6

A rare exception to the generally pricey and mediocre options that surround Plaza Mayor, Casa María combines professional service and a menu that effortlessly spans the modern and traditional. There's something for most tastes, with carefully chosen tapas, lunchtime stews and dishes such as sticky rice with lobster. ([📞]91 559 10 07; www.casamariaplazamayor.com; Plaza Mayor 23; tapas from €2.90, 4/6 tapas €11/16, mains €9-18; [🕐]noon-11pm; [M]Sol)

Restaurante Sobrino de Botín
CASTILIAN €€€

10 Map p28, D7

It's not every day that you can eat in the oldest restaurant in the world

---

Top Tip

Local Specialities

In addition to the chickpea-and-meat hotpot that is *cocido a la madrileña*, Taberna La Bola serves up other Madrid specialities such as *callos* (tripe) and *sopa castellana* (garlic soup).

Understand
Madrid & the Spanish Royal Family

Felipe II (r 1556–98) ascended to the Spanish throne at a time when Madrid was an obscure provincial outpost, home to just 30,000 people and dwarfed by Toledo, Seville and Valladolid. But Felipe II changed Madrid's fortunes forever in 1561 when he chose the city as Spain's capital and transformed it into the capital of an empire on which the sun never set.

Felipe V (r 1700–46) may have lost most of Spain's European possessions during the Europe-wide War of the Spanish Succession (1702–13), but he was the first monarch of the Bourbon dynasty, which still rules Spain today. His centralisation of state control and attempts at land reform began the process of transforming Spain into a modern European nation, and the former clearly cemented Madrid's claims as Spain's pre-eminent city. Felipe V also laid the plans for the Palacio Real (Royal Palace).

Carlos III (r 1759–88) came to be known as the best 'mayor' Madrid had ever had. He introduced Madrid's first program of sanitation and public hygiene, completed the Palacio Real, inaugurated the Real Jardín Botánico (Royal Botanical Garden) and embarked on a major road-building program. He also sponsored local and foreign artists, including Goya and Tiepolo.

Juan Carlos I (r 1976–2014) was a protégé of Franco, and the dictator's apparently loyal lieutenant, but when he took the throne aged just 37 two days after Franco died in July 1976, he oversaw Spain's transition to democracy. In 1981, a group of armed Guardia Civil led by Lt Col Antonio Tejero attempted a coup by occupying the parliament building. The king appeared on national television to denounce them and the coup collapsed.

Felipe VI (r 2014–) Spain's current king assumed the throne when his father, Juan Carlos I abdicated amid a series of scandals engulfing the royal family. This generational change, a break with the past and a more informal approach has played well with Spanish public opinion, although it remains to be seen whether this will continue at a time when much of Spain appears to have fallen out of love with its royal family.

(the *Guinness Book of Records* has recognised it as the oldest – established in 1725). The secret of its staying power is fine *cochinillo asado* (roast suckling pig; €25) and *cordero asado* (roast lamb; €25) cooked in wood-fired ovens. Eating in the vaulted cellar is a treat. (☎91 366 42 17; www.botin.es; Calle de los Cuchilleros 17; mains €19-27; ⊙1-4pm & 8pm-midnight; Ⓜ La Latina, Sol)

Drinking

Cafe de Oriente   CAFE

11 🚇 Map p28, B5

The outdoor tables of this distinguished old cafe are among the most sought-after in central Madrid, providing as they do a front-row seat for the beautiful Plaza de Oriente, with the Palacio Real as a backdrop. The building itself was once part of a long-gone, 17th-century convent and the interior feels a little like a set out of Mitteleuropa. (📞91 541 39 74; Plaza de Oriente 2; 🕐8.30am-1.30am Mon-Thu, 9am-2.30am Fri & Sat, 9am-1.30am Sun; 🚇Ópera)

🅠 Local Life
A Calamari Roll

One of the lesser-known culinary specialities of Madrid is a *bocadillo de calamares* (a small baguette-style roll filled to bursting with deep-fried calamari). You'll find them in many bars in the streets surrounding Plaza Mayor and neighbouring bars along Calle de los Botoneros, off Plaza Mayor's southeastern corner. Places include **La Ideal** (📞91 365 72 78; Calle de Botoneras 4; bocadillos €2.70; 🕐9am-11pm Sun-Thu, 9am-midnight Fri & Sat; 🚇Sol) and **La Campana** (📞91 364 29 84; www.calamareslacampana.com; Calle de Botoneras 6; bocadillos €2.70; 🕐9am-11pm Sun-Thu, 9am-midnight Fri & Sat; 🚇Sol). At around €2.70, it's the perfect street snack.

Café del Real   BAR

12 🚇 Map p28, C5

A cafe and cocktail bar in equal parts, this intimate place serves up creative coffees and cocktails to the soundtrack of chill-out music. The best seats are upstairs, where the low ceilings, wooden beams and leather chairs make for a great place to pass an afternoon with friends. (📞91 547 21 24; Plaza de Isabel II 2; 🕐8am-1am Mon-Thu, 8am-2.30am Fri, 9am-2.30am Sat, 10am-11.30pm Sun; 🚇Ópera)

The Sherry Corner   WINE BAR

13 🚇 Map p28, C6

The Sherry Corner, inside the Mercado de San Miguel, has found an excellent way to give a crash course in sherry. For €25, you get six small glasses of top-quality sherry to taste, each of which is matched to a different tapa. Guiding you through the process is an audioguide in eight languages (Spanish, English, German, French, Italian, Portuguese, Russian and Japanese). (📞681 007 700; www.sherry-corner.com; Stall 24, Mercado de San Miguel, Plaza de San Miguel; 🕐10am-9pm; 🚇Sol)

Chocolatería de San Ginés   CAFE

14 🚇 Map p28, D6

One of the grand icons of the Madrid night, this *chocolate con churros* cafe sees a sprinkling of tourists throughout the day, but locals pack it out in their search for sustenance on their way home from a nightclub somewhere close to dawn. Only in Madrid...

(📞 91 365 65 46; www.chocolateriasangines.com; Pasadizo de San Ginés 5; ⏰ 24hr; Ⓜ Sol)

Anticafé
CAFE

15 ☕ Map p28, C5

Bohemian kitsch in the best sense is the prevailing theme here and it runs right through the decor, regular cultural events and, of course, the clientele. As such, it won't be to everyone's taste, but we think that it adds some much-needed variety to the downtown drinking scene. (Calle de la Unión 2; ⏰ 5pm-2am Tue-Sun; Ⓜ Ópera)

Teatro Joy Eslava
CLUB

16 ☕ Map p28, D5

The only things guaranteed at this grand old Madrid dance club (housed in a 19th-century theatre) are a crowd and the fact that it'll be open (it claims to have operated every single day for the past 29 years). The music and the crowd are a mixed bag, but queues are long and invariably include locals and tourists, and even the occasional *famoso* (celebrity). (Joy Madrid; 📞 91 366 37 33; www.joy-eslava.com; Calle del Arenal 11; ⏰ 11.30pm-6am; Ⓜ Sol)

Charada
CLUB

17 ☕ Map p28, C3

Charada is a reliable regular on the Madrid clubbing scene. Its two rooms (one red, the other black) are New York chic with no hint of the building's former existence as a brothel. The cocktails are original and we especially like it when they turn their attention to electronica, but they also do disco and house. (📞 663 230 504; www.charada.es; Calle de la Bola 13; admission €12; ⏰ midnight-6am Wed-Sun; Ⓜ Santo Domingo)

Entertainment

Café de Chinitas
FLAMENCO

18 ⭐ Map p28, C3

One of the most distinguished *tablaos* (flamenco venues) in Madrid, drawing in everyone from the Spanish royal family to Bill Clinton, Café de Chinitas has an elegant setting and top-notch performers. It may attract loads of tourists, but flamenco aficionados also give it top marks. Reservations are highly recommended. (📞 91 547 15 02; www.chinitas.com; Calle de Torija 7; admission incl drink/meal €36/48; ⏰ shows 8pm & 10.30pm Mon-Sat; Ⓜ Santo Domingo)

Las Tablas
FLAMENCO

19 ⭐ Map p28, B2

Las Tablas has a reputation for quality flamenco and reasonable prices; it could just be the best choice in town. Most nights you'll see a classic flamenco show, with plenty of throaty singing and soul-baring dancing. Antonia Moya and Marisol Navarro, leading lights in the flamenco world, are regular performers here. (📞 91 542 05 20; www.lastablasmadrid.com; Plaza de España 9; admission incl drink €27; ⏰ shows 8pm & 10pm; Ⓜ Plaza de España)

Teatro Real   OPERA

20 ⭐ Map p28, C5

After spending €100 million-plus on a
long rebuilding project, the Teatro Real
is as technologically advanced as any
venue in Europe, and is the city's grandest stage for elaborate operas, ballets
and classical music. The cheapest seats
are so far away you'll need a telescope,
although the sound quality is consistent
throughout. (☑902 24 48 48; www.teatro-
real.com; Plaza de Oriente; Ⓜ Ópera)

Shopping

Antigua Casa Talavera   CERAMICS

21 🔒 Map p28, C3

The extraordinary tiled facade of this
wonderful old shop conceals an Aladdin's cave of ceramics from all over
Spain. This is not the mass-produced
stuff aimed at a tourist market, but

comes from the small family potters of
Andalucía and Toledo, ranging from
the decorative (tiles) to the useful
(plates, jugs and other kitchen items).
The old couple who run the place
are delightful. (☑91 547 34 17; www.
antiguacasatalavera.com; Calle de Isabel la
Católica 2; ⏱10am-1.30pm & 5-8pm Mon-Fri,
10am-1.30pm Sat; Ⓜ Santo Domingo)

El Arco Artesanía   HANDICRAFTS

22 🔒 Map p28, D6

This original shop in the southwestern
corner of Plaza Mayor sells an outstanding array of homemade designer
souvenirs, from stone, ceramic and
glass work to jewellery and home
fittings. The papier-mâché figures are
gorgeous, but there's so much else
here to turn your head. (☑913 65 26
80; www.artesaniaelarco.com; Plaza Mayor
9; ⏱10am-9pm Mon-Sat, 10am-5pm Sun;
Ⓜ Sol, La Latina)

Casa Hernanz   SHOES

23 🔒 Map p28, D7

Comfy, rope-soled *alpargatas* (espadrilles), Spain's traditional summer
footwear, are worn by everyone from
the King of Spain down, and you can
buy your own pair at this humble
workshop, which has been hand-
making the shoes for five generations;
you can even get them made to order.
Prices range from €5 to €40 and
queues form whenever the weather
starts to warm up. (☑91 36 65 450; www.
alpargateriahernanz.com; Calle de Toledo 18;
⏱9am-1.30pm & 4.30-8pm Mon-Fri, 10am-
2pm Sat; Ⓜ La Latina, Sol)

Ⓠ Local Life
Opera & Dinner

If you can't get tickets to your favourite opera, do what the locals do
and try the altogether less formal
atmosphere of **El Café de la Ópera**
(☑91 542 63 82; www.elcafedelaopera.
com; Calle de Arrieta 6; ⏱8am-midnight;
Ⓜ Ópera). Opposite the Teatro Real,
this classic before-performance
cafe has waiters who break into
song from around 9.30pm on Friday
and Saturday evenings, when you'll
fork out a minimum €45 for a meal.

CRISTINA ARIAS/GETTY IMAGES ©

Maty

El Flamenco Vive
FLAMENCO

24 🔒 Map p28, C6

This temple to flamenco has it all, from guitars and songbooks to well-priced CDs, polka-dotted dancing costumes, shoes, colourful plastic jewellery and literature about flamenco. It's the sort of place that will appeal as much to curious first timers as to serious students of the art. It also organises classes in flamenco guitar. (📞 91 547 39 17; www.elflamencovive. es; Calle Conde de Lemos 7; 🕙 10am-1.45pm & 5-9pm Mon-Fri, 10am-1.45pm & 5-9pm Sat & 1st Sun of month; Ⓜ Ópera)

Maty
FLAMENCO

25 🔒 Map p28, E5

Wandering around central Madrid, it's easy to imagine that flamenco outfits have been reduced to imitation dresses sold as souvenirs to tourists. That's why places like Maty matter. Here you'll find dresses, shoes and all the accessories that go with the genre, with sizes for children and adults. These are the real deal, with prices to match, but they make brilliant gifts. (📞 91 531 32 91; www.maty.es; Calle del Maestro Victoria 2; 🕙 10am-1.45pm & 4.30-8pm Mon-Fri, 10am-2pm & 4.30-8pm Sat & 1st Sun of month; Ⓜ Sol)

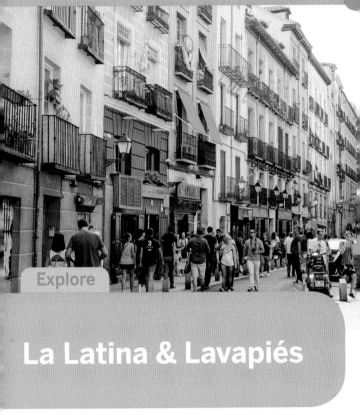

Explore

La Latina & Lavapiés

La Latina combines Madrid's best selection of tapas bars with a medieval streetscape studded with elegant churches. Calle de la Cava Baja could just be our favourite street in town for tapas. Multi-cultural Lavapiés is a world away, at once one of the city's oldest and most traditional *barrios* and home to more immigrants than any other central Madrid *barrio*.

The Sights in a Day

☀ The **Basílica de San Francisco El Grande** (p44) is one of Madrid's most imposing churches and its many treasures are a fine way to start the day. A walk up the hill through La Morería, medieval Madrid's Muslim quarter, takes you to **Iglesia de San Andrés** (p44) on lovely Plaza de la Paja. Enjoy lunch at **Almendro 13** (p41) and an early afternoon mojito at **Delic** (p41).

☀ The free **Museo de San Isidro** (p44) is one of Madrid's more rewarding museums. Shop for jewellery at **Helena Rohner** (p49), then meander down the hill to Lavapiés. A quiet drink high above it all at **Gau&Café** (p48) is a wonderful way to pass an afternoon.

☾ Return up the hill to Calle de la Cava Baja and its surrounding streets. **Taberna Tempranillo** (p48) captures the spirit of the *barrio,* but anywhere along this iconic street is as good for pre-dinner tapas as it is for a drink. Follow a flamenco show at **Casa Patas** (p48) with dinner at **Posada de la Villa** (p48), then dance the night away at **ContraClub** (p49).

For a local's day at El Rastro flea market, see p40.

🔍 Local Life
El Rastro Sunday (p40)

♥ Best of La Latina & Lavapiés

Tapas
Juana La Loca (p45)

Txirimiri (p41)

Almendro 13 (p41)

Taberna Matritum (p44)

Churches
Basílica de San Francisco El Grande (p44)

Iglesia de San Andrés (p44)

Shopping
El Rastro (p40)

Helena Rohner (p49)

Caramelos Paco (p49)

Getting There

Ⓜ **Metro** La Latina (line 5) and Lavapiés (line 3) deposit you in the heart of these two *barrios*. Otherwise, Tirso de Molina (line 1) and Antón Martín (line 1) on the neighbourhood's northeastern fringe are the only others that are useful.

Local Life
El Rastro Sunday

There are few more enduring Madrid traditions than visiting El Rastro, believed to be Europe's largest flea market, on a Sunday. But El Rastro is so much more than a market: it's the prelude to an afternoon of vermouth and tapas in the bars of La Latina. Join the eating and drinking throngs, and you'll fulfil a key criteria of being considered a local.

❶ El Rastro

You could easily spend a Sunday morning inching your way down the Calle de la Ribera de los Curtidores, the street that hosts **El Rastro** (⊘8am-3pm Sun; Ⓜ La Latina). Cheap clothes, old flamenco records, even older photos of Madrid, faux designer purses, grungy T-shirts and household goods are the main fare. For every 10 pieces of junk, there's a real gem (a lost masterpiece, an Underwood typewriter...).

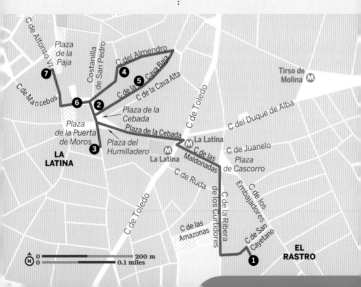

❷ Vermouth Hour

Sunday. One o'clock in the afternoon. A busy bar along Calle de la Cava Baja. Welcome to *la hora del vermut* (vermouth hour), a long-standing Madrid tradition whereby friends and families enjoy a post-Rastro aperitif. This tradition is deeply engrained in *madrileño* culture and most such bars are along or just off Calle de la Cava Baja.

❸ Txirimiri

Every local has a favourite place for ordering a *pincho de tortilla* (a *tapa* of *tortilla de patatas*, the quintessentially Spanish potato omelette). But food critics and your average punter alike are drawn in ever-increasing numbers to the Basque bar **Txirimiri** (Map p42, C3; ☎91 364 11 96; www.txirimiri. es; Calle del Humilladero 6; tapas from €4; ☺noon-4.30pm & 8.30pm-midnight Mon-Sat, closed Aug; Ⓜ La Latina). The tortilla is moist, it's impossible to stop at one, and it's utterly delicious.

❹ Almendro 13

Almendro 13 (☎91 365 42 52; Calle del Almendro 13; mains €7-15; ☺1-4pm & 7.30pm-midnight Sun-Thu, 1-5pm & 8pm-1am Fri & Sat; Ⓜ La Latina) is a wildly popular *taberna* where you come for traditional Spanish tapas with an emphasis on quality rather than frilly elaborations. Cured meats, cheeses, omelettes and many variations on these themes dominate the menu; the famously good *huevos rotos* (literally, 'broken eggs') served with *jamón* (ham) and thin potato slices is the star.

❺ Casa Lucas

Casa Lucas (☎91 365 08 04; www. casalucas.es; Calle de la Cava Baja 30; tapas/raciónes from €5/12; ☺1-3.30pm & 8pm-midnight Thu-Tue, 1-3.30pm Wed; Ⓜ La Latina) takes a sideways glance at traditional Spanish tapas, then heads off in new directions. There is a range of hot and cold tapas and larger *raciónes*. The menu changes regularly as the chef comes up with new ideas, and particular attention is paid to the wine list.

❻ Plaza de San Andrés

While half of Madrid filters out across the city, either heading home or to the Parque del Buen Retiro, the remainder hang out in the Plaza de San Andrés, with its storeys-high mural and fine church backdrop. As the sun nears the horizon, the light softens and the gathered hordes start the drumbeats and begin to dance.

❼ Delic

We could go on for hours about **Delic** (☎91 364 54 50; www.delic.es; Costanilla de San Andrés 14; ☺11am-2am Sun & Tue-Thu, 11am-2.30am Fri & Sat; Ⓜ La Latina), a long-standing cafe-bar, but we'll reduce it to its most basic elements: nursing an exceptionally good mojito (€8) or three on a warm summer's evening at Delic's outdoor tables on one of Madrid's prettiest plazas is one of life's great pleasures. Bliss.

Parque de Atenas

Parque del Emir Mohamed I

Viaduct

Jardines de las Vistillas

Plaza de Gabriel Miró

Plaza del Alamillo

C de la Morería

C de Alfonso VI

Plaza del Príncipe Anglona

Jardín del Príncipe Anglona

C del Príncipe Anglona

C del Rollo

C del Conde

Plaza del Cordón

C de San Justo

C de Segovia

Plaza del Conde de Barajas

C de la Pasa

Plaza de Puerta Cerrada

Plaza de Segovia Nueva

14

Plaza de Granado

Plaza de la Paja

Costanilla de San Pedro

C del Nuncio

C del Almendro

8

15

C de Grafal

10

Plaza de Redondilla

La Morería

Museo de San Isidro

9

C de la Cava Baja

C de la Cava Alta

4

C de Yeseros

C de Bailén

C de Don Pedro

Iglesia de San Andrés

2

3

Plaza de San Andrés

12

C de Toledo

C de los Estudios

17

C de la Morería

C de San Buenaventura

Plaza de la Puerta de Moros

Plaza del Humilladero

Plaza de la Cebada

C de San Milán

Plaza de San Francisco

Carrera de San Francisco

C de San Isidro Labrador

6

5

C de Oriente

C de Humilladero

La Latina Ⓜ

Ⓜ **La Latina**

Plaza de Cascorro

1

Basílica de San Francisco El Grande

C de las Aguas

LA LATINA

C de Luciente

C de la Cebada

C de Ruda

7

C del Rosario

C del Ángel

16

C del Mediodía Grande

C de Toledo

C de Santa Ana

Plaza General Vara del Rey

EL RASTRO

C de Calatrava

C del Mediodía Chica

C de la Paloma

C Mira el Río Alta

El Rastro

C de las Amazonas

C de la Ribera de los Curtidores

Gran Vía de San Francisco

C de la Ventosa

C de Toledo

C de Capitan San Martinez

C del Carnero

C Arganzuela

C Mira el Río Baja

C de Carlos Arniches

Plaza Campillo del Mundo Nuevo

Glorieta de Puerta de Toledo

Ⓜ **Puerta de Toledo**

Ronda de Toledo

E

C Salvador

C de Atocha

de la Concepción Jerónima

F

Plaza de Jacinto Benavente

C del Conde de Romanones

C del Doctor Cortezo

C de los Relatores

C de Luiz Vélez de Guevera

G

C de las Huertas

13

C de Cañizares

H

HUERTAS

Plaza de Matute

C de León

C de la Colegiada

Tirso de Molina

Plaza de Tirso de Molina

Tirso de Molina

C de la Magdalena

Antón Martín

Plaza de Antón Martín

del Duque de Alba

C de la Espada

C Soler y González

C de la Cabeza

C de la Torrecilla del Leal

C de Juanelo

C del Calvario

C del Olmo

C de la Encomienda

C de Jesús y María

C de Ministriles

C del Olivar

C del Ave María

C Tres Peces

C de las dos Hermanas

C de San Carlos

C de Abades

C de la Esperanza

de San Cayetano

C del Oso

LAVAPIÉS

C de Lavapiés

C del Ave María

C de Primavera

C de Buena Vista

C de Zurita

C de Fray Ceferino Gonzalez

C de Cabesteros

C de Mesón de Paredes

C del Amparo

C de Salitre

C de la Fé

C de Rodás

C de los Embajadores

C del Sombrete

Plaza de Lavapiés

Lavapiés

C de Argumosa

C de la Huerta del Bayo

C de Ventorrillo

C de Santiago Verde

C de Tribulete

C de la Sombrería

C Mira el Sol

11

C de Espino

C de Miguel Servet

C de Valencia

C del Doctor Fourquet

C del Casino

C Provisiones

Sights

Basílica de San Francisco El Grande   CHURCH

1 ⊙ Map p42, A3

Lording it over the southwestern corner of La Latina, this imposing and recently restored baroque basilica is one of Madrid's grandest old churches. Its extravagantly frescoed dome is, by some estimates, the largest in Spain and the fourth largest in the world, with a height of 56m and diameter of 33m. (Plaza de San Francisco 1; adult/concession €3/2; ☉mass 8-10.30am Mon-Sat, museum 10.30am-12.30pm & 4-6pm Tue-Sun Sep-Jun, 10.30am-12.30pm & 5-7pm Tue-Sun Jul & Aug; Ⓜ La Latina, Puerta de Toledo)

Iglesia de San Andrés   CHURCH

2 ⊙ Map p42, B2

This proud church is more impos-ing than beautiful and what you see today is the result of restoration work completed after the church was gut-ted during the civil war. Stern, dark columns with gold-leaf capitals against the rear wall lead your eyes up into

---

✅ Top Tip

San Francisco El Grande

Although entry to the Basílica de San Francisco El Grande is free dur-ing morning Mass times, there is no access to the museum and the lights in the Capilla de San Bernardino won't be on to illuminate the Goya.

---

the dome – all rose, yellow and green, rich with sculpted floral fantasies and cherubs poking out of every nook and cranny. (Plaza de San Andrés 1; ☉8am-1pm & 6-8pm Mon-Sat, 8am-1pm Sun; Ⓜ La Latina)

Museo de San Isidro   MUSEUM

3 ⊙ Map p42, C2

This engaging museum occupies the spot where San Isidro Labrador ended his days around 1172. A particular highlight is the large model based on Pedro Teixeira's famous 1656 map of Madrid. Of great historical interest (though not much to look at) is the 'miraculous well', where the saint called forth water to slake his master's thirst. In another miracle, the son of the saint's master fell into a well, whereupon Isidro prayed and prayed until the water rose and lifted his son to safety. (Museo de los Orígenes; ☎91 366 74 15; www.madrid.es; Plaza de San Andrés 2; admission free; ☉9.30am-8pm Tue-Sun Sep-Jul, 9.30am-2.30pm Tue-Fri, 9.30am-8pm Sat & Sun Aug; Ⓜ La Latina)

Eating

Taberna Matritum   MODERN SPANISH €€

4 🍴 Map p42, D2

This little gem is reason enough to detour from the more popular Calle de la Cava Baja next door. The seasonal menu here encompasses terrific tapas, salads and generally creative cook-ing – try the *cocido* croquettes or the

FEARGUS COONEY/GETTY IMAGES ©

Basílica de San Francisco El Grande

winter *calçots* (large spring onions) from Catalonia. The wine list runs into the hundreds and it's sophisticated without being pretentious. Highly recommended. (☎91 365 82 37; Calle de la Cava Alta 17; mains €12-22; ◷1.30-4pm & 8.30pm-midnight Wed-Sun, 8.30pm-midnight Mon & Tue; Ⓜ La Latina)

Txirimiri
TAPAS €€

5 ⓧ Map p42, C3

This *pintxos* (Basque tapas) bar is a great little discovery just down from the main La Latina tapas circuit. Wonderful wines, gorgeous *pinchos* (snacks; the *tortilla de patatas* – potato and onion omelette – is superb) and fine risottos add up to a pretty

special combination. (☎91 364 11 96; www.txirimiri.es; Calle del Humilladero 6; tapas from €4; ◷noon-4.30pm & 8.30pm-midnight Mon-Sat, closed Aug; Ⓜ La Latina)

Juana La Loca
TAPAS €€

6 ⓧ Map p42, B3

Juana La Loca does a range of creative tapas with tempting options lined up along the bar, and more on the menu that they prepare to order. But we love it above all for its *tortilla de patatas*, which is distinguished from others of its kind by the caramelised onions – simply wonderful. (☎91 364 05 25; Plaza de la Puerta de Moros 4; tapas from €5, mains €8-19; ◷noon-1am Tue-Sun, 8pm-1am Mon; Ⓜ La Latina)

Understand

Tapas: A Primer

Many would argue that tapas are Spain's greatest culinary gift to the world. While devotees of paella and *jamón* (ham) can make a convincing counterclaim, what clinches it for us is the fact that the potential variety of tapas is endless.

Anything can be a *tapa* (a single item of tapas), from a handful of olives or a slice of *jamón* on bread to a *tortilla de patatas* (Spanish potato omelette) served in liquefied form. That's because tapas is the canvas upon which Spanish chefs paint the story of a nation's obsession with food, the means by which they show their fidelity to traditional Spanish tastes even as they gently nudge their compatriots in previously unimagined directions. By making the most of very little, tapas serves as a link to the impoverished Madrid of centuries past. By re-imagining even the most sacred Spanish staples, tapas is the culinary trademark of a confident country rushing headlong into the future.

Tapas Etiquette

To many visitors, ordering tapas can seem like one of the dark arts of Spanish etiquette. Fear not: in many bars in Madrid, it couldn't be easier. With so many tapas varieties lined up along the bar, you either take a small plate and help yourself or point to the morsel you want. In such cases, it's customary to keep track of what you eat (by holding on to the toothpicks for example) and then tell the bar staff how many you've had when it's time to pay. Otherwise, many places have a list of tapas, either on a menu or posted up behind the bar. If you can't choose, ask for *'la especialidad de la casa'* (the house speciality) and it's hard to go wrong. Another way of eating tapas is to order *raciones* (literally 'rations'; large tapas servings) or *media raciones* (half-rations; smaller tapas servings). These plates and half-plates of a particular dish are a good way to go if you particularly like something and want more than a mere *tapa*. Remember, however, that after one or two *raciones* most people are almost certainly full.

Malacatín
MADRILEÑO €€

7 Map p42, D3

If you want to see *madrileños* enjoying their favourite local food, this is one of the best places to do so. The clamour of conversation bounces off the tiled walls of the cramped dining area adorned with bullfighting memorabilia. The speciality is as much *cocido* as you can eat (€20). (📞91 365 52 41; www.malacatin.com; Calle de Ruda 5; mains €11-15; ⏱11am-5.30pm Mon-Wed & Sat, 11am-5.30pm Thu & Fri, closed Aug; Ⓜ La Latina)

Enotaberna del León de Oro
SPANISH €€

8 Map p42, D1

The stunning restoration work that brought to life the **Posada del León de Oro** (📞91 119 14 94; www.posadadelleonde oro.com; Calle de la Cava Baja 12; r from €105; ❄ 🛜; Ⓜ La Latina) also bequeathed to La Latina a fine new bar-restaurant. The emphasis is on matching carefully chosen wines with creative dishes (such as baby squid with potato emulsion and rucula pesto) in a casual atmosphere. There are also plenty of gins to choose from. It's a winning combination. (📞91 119 14 94; www.posada delleondeoro.com; Calle de la Cava Baja 12; tapas from €3.50 mains €14-20; ⏱1-4pm & 8pm-midnight; Ⓜ La Latina)

Casa Lucio
SPANISH €€€

9 Map p42, C2

Lucio has been wowing *madrileños* with his light touch, quality ingredients and home-style local cooking since 1974 – think eggs (a Lucio speciality) and roasted meats in abundance. There's also *rabo de toro* (bull's tail) during the Fiestas de San Isidro Labrador and plenty of *rioja* (red wine) to wash away the mere thought of it. (📞91 365 82 17, 91 365 32 52; www.casalucio.es; Calle de la Cava Baja 35; mains €18-28; ⏱1-4pm & 8.30pm-midnight, closed Aug; Ⓜ La Latina)

Local Life
Sardines at El Rastro

There are few more enduring local traditions than *sardinas a la plancha* (sardines cooked on the grill) at **Bar Santurce** (📞646 238303; www. barsanturce.com; Plaza General Vara del Rey 14; bocadillos from €2.50, raciones from €3.90; ⏱9am-3pm Tue-Sun; Ⓜ La Latina); during El Rastro it can be difficult to even get near the bar. Then step next door to the tiny and equally beloved **Aceitunas Jiménez** (📞91 365 46 23; Plaza del General Vara del Rey 14; ⏱10.30am-2.30pm & 3.30-8pm Mon-Thu, 10.30am-2.30pm Fri & Sat, 10.30am-3pm Sun; Ⓜ La Latina), purveyor of pickled olives, eggplants, garlic and anything else they've decided to pickle, served in plastic cups.

Posada de la Villa
MADRILEÑO €€€

10 Map p42, D2

This wonderfully restored 17th-century *posada* (inn) is something of a local landmark. The atmosphere is formal, the decoration sombre and traditional (heavy timber and brick-work), and the cuisine decidedly local – roast meats, *cocido*, *callos* (tripe) and *sopa de ajo* (garlic soup). (☎91 366 18 80; www.posadadelavilla.com; Calle de la Cava Baja 9; mains €19-28; ⏱1-4pm & 8pm-midnight Mon-Sat, 1-4pm Sun, closed Aug; ⓜLa Latina)

Local Life
Late in Lavapiés

Not many tourists make it down the Lavapiés hill and those that do tend to leave before darkness falls. If you're still around, **La Inquilina** (☎91 468 25 33; www.lainquilina.es; Calle del Ave María 39; ⏱7pm-2.30am Tue-Thu, 7pm-3am Fri, 1pm-2.30am Sat & Sun; ⓜLavapiés) is one of the *barrio's* coolest bars, while **Nuevo Café de Barbieri** (☎91 527 36 58; Calle del Ave María 45; ⏱4pm-1am Tue-Thu, 4pm-2am Fri & Sat, 4-11pm Sun; ⓜLavapiés), a few doors down, is a neighbour-hood classic. And for late-night comfort food, try the *croquetas* at legendary **Bar Melo's** (☎91 527 50 54; Calle del Ave María; mains from €7.50; ⏱2.30pm-1.30am Tue-Sat, closed Aug; ⓜLavapiés).

Drinking

Gau&Café
CAFE

11 Map p42, F5

Decoration that's light and airy, with pop-art posters of Audrey Hepburn and James Bond. A large terrace with views over the Lavapiés rooftops. A stunning backdrop of a ruined church atop which the cafe sits. With so much else going for it, it almost seems in-cidental that it also serves great teas, coffees and snacks (as well as meals). (www.gaucafe.com; 4th fl, Calle de Tribulete 14; ⏱11am-midnight Mon-Fri, 1.30pm-midnight Sat; ⓜLavapiés)

Taberna Tempranillo
WINE BAR

12 Map p42, C2

You could come here for the tapas, but we recommend Taberna Tempranillo primarily for its wines, of which it has a selection that puts numerous Spanish bars to shame; many wines are sold by the glass. It's not a late-night place, but it's always packed in the early evening and on Sundays after El Rastro. (Calle de la Cava Baja 38; ⏱1-3.30pm & 8pm-midnight Tue-Sun, 8pm-midnight Mon; ⓜLa Latina)

Entertainment

Casa Patas
FLAMENCO

13 Map p42, G2

One of the top flamenco stages in Madrid, this *tablao* (flamenco venue) always offers flawless quality that serves as a good introduction to the art. It's not the friendliest place in town, especially if you're only here for the show, and you're likely to be crammed in a little, but no one complains about the standard of the performances. (📞91 369 04 96; www.casa patas.com; Calle de Cañizares 10; admission incl drink €36; ⏱shows 10.30pm Mon-Thu, 9pm & midnight Fri & Sat; Ⓜ Antón Martín, Tirso de Molina)

ContraClub LIVE MUSIC

14 ⭐ Map p42, A2

ContraClub is a crossover live music venue and nightclub, with an eclectic mix of live music (pop, rock, indie, singer-songwriter, blues...). After the live acts (from 10pm), the resident DJs serve up equally diverse beats (indie, pop, funk and soul) to make sure you don't move elsewhere. (📞91 365 55 45; www.contraclub.es; Calle de Bailén 16; admission €6-15; ⏱10pm-6am Wed-Sat; Ⓜ La Latina)

Shopping

Helena Rohner JEWELLERY

15 🔒 Map p42, D2

One of Europe's most creative jewellery designers, Helena Rohner has a spacious boutique in La Latina. Working with silver, stone, porcelain, wood and Murano glass, she makes inventive pieces and her work is a regular feature of Paris fashion shows. In her own words, she seeks to recreate 'the magic of Florence, the vitality of London and the luminosity of Madrid'. (📞91 365 79 06; www.helenarohner.com.es; Calle del Almendro 4; ⏱9am-8.30pm Mon-Fri, noon-2.30pm & 3.30-8pm Sat, noon-3pm Sun; Ⓜ La Latina, Tirso de Molina)

Botería Julio Rodríguez HANDICRAFTS

16 🔒 Map p42, B3

One of the last makers of traditional Spanish wineskins left in Madrid, Botería Julio Rodríguez is like a window on a fast-disappearing world. They make a great gift and, as you'd expect, they're in a different league from the cheap wineskins found in souvenir shops across downtown Madrid. (📞91 365 66 29; www.boteriajulio rodriguez.es; Calle del Águila 12; ⏱9.30am-2pm & 4.30-8pm Mon-Fri, 10am-1.30pm Sat; Ⓜ La Latina)

Caramelos Paco FOOD

17 🔒 Map p42, D2

A sweet shop that needs to be seen to be believed, Caramelos Paco has been indulging children and adults alike since 1934 and it remains unrivalled when it comes to variety. There's almost nothing you can't find here and even the shop window is a work of art. (📞91 365 42 58, 91 354 06 70; www.caramelospaco.com; Calle de Toledo 53-55; ⏱9.30am-2pm & 5-8.30pm Mon-Fri, 9.30am-2pm Sat, 11am-3pm Sun; Ⓜ La Latina)

Explore

Sol, Santa Ana & Huertas

The downtown streets around the Plaza de la Puerta del Sol are the sum total of all Madrid's personalities, and it's here that the world of *madrileños* most often intersects with that of visitors. Away to the southeast, Plaza de Santa Ana and Huertas combine a stately charm with terrific restaurants and nightlife whose noise reverberates out across the city.

The Sights in a Day

☼ Start your day in Plaza de Santa Ana, one of the city's liveliest and most agreeable squares. Spend an hour or two wandering the **Barrio de las Letras** (p56), then take in the **Real Academia de Bellas Artes de San Fernando** (p55), one of Madrid's most underrated art galleries. For lunch, try **La Finca de Susana** (p57).

☼ Try to track down the trail of Cervantes in the Barrio de las Letras, pause for designer tapas at **Vi Cool** (p57), and indulge yourself with a sumptuous Arab bath at **Hammam al-Andalus** (p56).

☾ Begin this rather long evening with a sherry at wonderful **La Venencia** (p59), before embarking on a tapas crawl via **Casa Alberto** (p57) and **Los Gatos** (p58). Consider Madrid's home of live jazz, **Café Central** (p62), or a flamenco show at **Villa Rosa** (p62). Whichever you choose, follow it up with a cocktail or two at **El Imperfecto** (p60). Aesthetes will enjoy the cool rooftop sophistication of **La Terraza del Urban** (p60).

For a local's night out in Huertas, see p52.

🔍 Local Life

A Night Out in Huertas (p52)

🖤 Best of Sol, Santa Ana & Huertas

Eating
Casa Alberto (p57)

Vi Cool (p57)

Ramiro's Tapas Wine Bar (p58)

Los Gatos (p58)

La Terraza del Casino (p58)

Bars
La Venencia (p59)

El Imperfecto (p60)

La Terraza del Urban (p60)

The Roof (p53)

Live Music
Café Central (p62)

Villa Rosa (p62)

Costello Café & Niteclub (p63)

Sala El Sol (p62)

Cardamomo (p53)

Getting There

Ⓜ **Metro** Sol station (lines 1, 2, 3) is the most convenient, followed by Sevilla (line 2), Gran Vía (lines 1, 5), Antón Martín (line 1), Banco de España (line 2) and Atocha (line 1).

Local Life
A Night Out in Huertas

As sunset nears, locals begin arriving in the Plaza de Santa Ana and the streets towards Sol and down towards the Paseo del Prado. That's because bars here range from cool and classy rooftop perches to ancient *barrio* classics that haven't changed in decades. And thrown in for good measure is arguably Madrid's finest collection of live-music venues.

❶ Plaza de Santa Ana

So many Huertas nights begin on this iconic Madrid square, surrounded as it is by so many bars with outdoor tables. Start wherever there's a free table on the square, but **Cervecería Alemana** (☏91 429 70 33; www.cerveceriaalemana.com; Plaza de Santa Ana 6; ⊙11am-12.30am Sun-Thu, to 2am Fri & Sat, closed Aug; Ⓜ Antón Martín, Sol) has a Hemingway history.

❷ Taberna La Dolores

Old bottles and beer mugs line the shelves at this Madrid institution. The 30-something crowd often includes the odd *famoso* (celebrity) or two. **Taberna La Dolores** (✆91 429 22 43; Plaza de Jesús 4; ⏱11am-1am; Ⓜ Antón Martín) claims to be 'the most famous bar in Madrid' – it's invariably full, so who are we to argue?

❸ Maceiras

Key to surviving long Madrid nights is never to drink on an empty stomach, and the Galician tapas (think octopus, green peppers) in **Maceiras** (✆91 429 15 84; Calle de las Huertas 66; mains €7-14; ⏱1.15-4.15pm & 8.30pm-midnight Mon-Sat, to 11.30pm Sun; Ⓜ Antón Martín), a rustic bar down the Huertas hill, are outstanding. Wash it down with a crisp white Ribeiro and you're halfway to being a local.

❹ Jazz Bar

Jazz aficionados begin the night at **Jazz Bar** (✆91 429 70 31; Calle de Moratín 35; ⏱3pm-2.30am; Ⓜ Antón Martín) before heading on to live performances elsewhere. With an endless jazz soundtrack, discreet leather booths and plenty of greenery, it's not surprising many return later in the night.

❺ Populart

Populart (✆91 429 84 07; www.populart. es; Calle de las Huertas 22; admission free; ⏱6pm-2.30am Sun-Thu, to 3.30am Fri & Sat, concerts 10pm; Ⓜ Antón Martín, Sol) offers low-key atmosphere and top-quality music, which is mostly jazz, with occasional blues, swing and even flamenco. Compay Segundo, Sonny Fortune and the Canal Street Jazz Band have all played here.

❻ Casa Pueblo

A storied Huertas bar that prides itself on free live jazz and a bohemian outlook, **Casa Pueblo** (✆91 420 20 38; Calle de León 3; ⏱5pm-2am Mon-Thu, 5pm-3am Fri, 3pm-3am Sat, 3pm-2am Sun; Ⓜ Antón Martín, Banco de España) is an agreeable bar serving up a winning combination of cakes and cocktails, and draws an in-the-know 30-something crowd.

❼ Cardamomo

One of the better flamenco stages in town, **Cardamomo** (✆91 805 10 38; www.cardamomo.es; Calle de Echegaray 15; ⏱10pm-3.30am, live shows 8pm & 10pm Wed-Mon; Ⓜ Sol, Sevilla) draws more tourists than aficionados, but the flamenco is top-notch and the darkened atmosphere carries a whiff of flamenco authenticity. The early show lasts 50 minutes, the later 90 minutes.

❽ The Roof

Seven floors above the Plaza de Santa Ana, **The Roof** (✆91 701 60 20; www. memadrid.com; Plaza de Santa Ana 14; ⏱9pm-1.30am Mon-Thu, 8pm-3am Fri & Sat; Ⓜ Antón Martín, Sol), a sybaritic open-air cocktail bar, has terrific views over Madrid's rooftops. It's a place for sophisticates, with chill-out areas with cushions, funky DJs and a dress policy designed to sort out the classy from the wannabes.

Plaza de Santa María Soledad

C del Desengaño

C del Barco

C del Valverde

C de Fuencarral

C de Hortaleza

Plaza de Vásquez de Mella

C de la Libertad

Gran Vía

0   200 m
0   0.1 miles

Plaza del Rey

C de la Salud

C de las Tres Cruces

C de Chinchilla

Gran Vía

Plaza de la Red de San Luis

C del Caballero de Gracia

C de las Infantas

C de Clavel

C de la Reina

C del Marqués de Valdeiglesias

Banco de España

C de la Abada

C del Carmen

C de Preciados

C Galdó

Plaza del Carmen

C de San Alberto

C de la Montera

CENTRO

C de los Jardines

⭐ 25   27

C de la Aduana

C de la Virgen de los Peligros

Edificio Grassy

◉ 4

Edificio Metrópolis ◉ 5   C de Alca

Sevilla Ⓜ

◉ 2

Banco Espa

Real Academia de Bellas Artes de San Fernando

✖ 1

15 ✖

C de Alcalá

C de Sevilla

Círculo de Bellas Artes

C de los Madrazo

C de Marq de Casa R

Plaza de la Puerta del Sol

Sol Ⓜ 🅿

◉ 3   28

Sevilla Ⓜ

C de los Cedaceros

8 ◉

C del Arenal

Plaza de Canalejas

C de Arlabán

✖ 9

C de Zorrilla

24 ⭐

C Mayor

C del Correo

C de la Paz

🅿 29

C de Cádiz

C de Espoz y Mina

C de Carretas

C de la Victoria

C de la Cruz

16 ✖

21 ⓘ

C del Pozo

20 ⓘ

Carrera de San Jerónimo

C de Ventura de la Vega

Carrera de San Jerónim

C de Fernánflor

Plaza de las Cortes

Carrera de San Jerónimo

SOL

C del Príncipe

C de Echegaray

18 ⓘ

Plaza de Jacinto Benavente

7 ◉

Hammam al-Andalus

C de la Concepción Jerónima

C del Doctor Cortezo

C de los Relatores

C de Barcelona

C de Luiz Vélez de Guevara

26 ⭐

Callejón de Álvarez Gato

Plaza de Santa Ana

Plaza del Ángel

23 ⭐

C de Manuel Fernández y González

30 ✖

C de León

14 ✖

C del Prado

6 ⓘ

C de San Agustín

Barrio de las Letras

C de Medinaceli

C de Cervantes

Plaz de Jes

17 ⓘ

C de Lope de Vega

13 ✖

C del

11 ✖

Plaza de Matute

10 ✖
12 ⓘ

19 ⓘ

HUERTAS

C del Olivar

C de Santa María

C de Atocha

C del Amor de Dios

22 ⓘ

C de las Huertas

Antón Martín Ⓜ

Plaza de Antón Martín

C de Moratín

C de la Magdalena

C de la Cabeza

C de Santa Isabel

Antón Martín Ⓜ

LAVAPIÉS

C del Ave María

C del Olmo

C de Fúcar

For reviews see

◉ Sights	p55
✖ Eating	p57
ⓘ Drinking	p59
⭐ Entertainment	p62
🅿 Shopping	p63

View from Círculo de Bellas Artes; sculpture: *Minerva,* by Juan Luis Vassallo

Sights

Real Academia de Bellas Artes de San Fernando   MUSEUM

1 🎯 Map p54, B2

Madrid's 'other' art gallery, the Real Academia de Bellas Artes has played a pivotal role in the artistic life of the city for centuries. As the royal fine arts academy, it has nurtured local talent, thereby complementing the royal penchant for drawing the great international artists of the day into their realm. The pantheon of former alumni reads like a Who's Who of Spanish art, and the collection that now hangs on the academy's walls is a suitably rich one. (📞91 524 08 64; www.realacademia bellasartessanfernando.com; Calle de Alcalá 13; adult/child €6/free, Wed free; 🕙10am-3pm Tue-Sun Sep-Jul; Ⓜ Sol, Sevilla)

Círculo de Bellas Artes   ARTS CENTRE, VIEWPOINT

2 🎯 Map p54, D2

For some of Madrid's best views, take the lift to the 7th floor of the 'Fine Arts Circle'. You can almost reach out and touch the glorious dome of the Edificio Metrópolis and otherwise take in Madrid in all its finery, including the distant mountains. Two bars, lounge music and places to recline add to the experience. Downstairs, the centre has exhibitions, concerts, short films and book readings.

Top Tip

It's Free

The Real Academia de Bellas Artes de San Fernando (p55) has a collection the envy of many a European gallery, and it's free to enjoy if you come on a Wednesday.

There's also a fine *belle-époque* **cafe** (☑91 521 69 42; ☺9am-1am Sun-Thu, to 3am Fri & Sat; Ⓜ Sevilla) on the ground floor. (La Azotea; ☑91 360 54 00; www. circulobellasartes.com; Calle de Alcalá 42; admission centre/roof terrace €1/4; ☺roof terrace 9am-2am Mon-Thu, 9am-2.30am Fri, 11am-2.30am Sat & Sun; Ⓜ Banco de España)

Plaza de la Puerta del Sol
SQUARE

3 ◎ Map p54, A3

The official centre point of Spain is a gracious, crowded hemisphere of elegant facades. It is, above all, a crossroads: people here are forever heading somewhere else, on foot, by metro (three lines cross here) or by bus (many lines terminate and start nearby). Hard as it is to believe now, in Madrid's earliest days, the Puerta del Sol (Gate of the Sun) was the eastern gate of the city. (Ⓜ Sol)

Edificio Grassy
ARCHITECTURE

4 ◎ Map p54, D2

Edificio Grassy, with the Rolex sign, was built in 1916. With its circular 'temple' as a crown, and profusion of

arcs and slender columns, it's one of the most elegant buildings along Gran Vía. (Gran Vía 1; Ⓜ Banco de España)

Edificio Metrópolis
ARCHITECTURE

5 ◎ Map p54, D2

Among the more interesting buildings along Gran Vía is the stunning, French-designed Edificio Metrópolis, built in 1905, which marks the southern end of Gran Vía. The winged victory statue atop its dome was added in 1975 and is best seen from Calle de Alcalá or Plaza de la Cibeles. (Gran Vía; Ⓜ Banco de España)

Barrio de las Letras
NEIGHBOURHOOD

6 ◎ Map p54, D4

The area that unfurls down the hill east of Plaza de Santa Ana is referred to as the Barrio de las Letras (District of Letters) because of the writers who lived here during Spain's golden age of the 16th and 17th centuries. Miguel de Cervantes Saavedra (1547–1616), the author of *Don Quijote,* spent much of his adult life in Madrid and lived and died at Calle de Cervantes 2 (Antón Martín); a plaque (dating from 1834) sits above the door. (Ⓜ Antón Martín)

Hammam al-Andalus
SPA

7 ◎ Map p54, A4

Housed in the excavated cellars of old Madrid, this imitation of a traditional Arab bath offers massages and aromatherapy beneath graceful arches, accompanied by the sound of trickling water. Prices are cheapest from 10am to 4pm Monday to Friday; reservations are required. There's also a Moroccan-style tearoom and restaurant upstairs. (☑91 429 90 20; madrid. hammamalandalus.com; Calle de Atocha 14; treatments €30-73; ☉10am-midnight; Ⓜ Sol)

Eating

Casa Labra   TAPAS €

8 Ⓧ Map p54, A3

Casa Labra has been going strong since 1860, an era that the decor strongly evokes. Locals love their *bacalao* (cod) and ordering it here – either as deep-fried tapas (*una tajada de bacalao* goes for €1.30) or as *una croqueta de bacalao* (croquette) – is a Madrid rite of initiation. As the lunchtime queues attest, they go through more than 700kg of cod every week. (☑91 532 14 05; www. casalabra.es; Calle de Tetuán 11; tapas from €1.25; ☉11.30am-3.30pm & 6-11pm; Ⓜ Sol)

La Finca de Susana   SPANISH €

9 Ⓧ Map p54, C3

It's difficult to find a better combination of price, quality cooking and classy atmosphere anywhere in Huertas. The softly lit dining area is bathed in greenery and the sometimes innovative, sometimes traditional food draws a hip young crowd. The duck confit with plums, turnips and couscous is a fine choice. No reservations. (☑91 369 35 57; www.grupandilana.

com/es/restaurantes/la-finca-de-susana; Calle de Arlabán 4; mains €7-12; ☉1-3.45pm & 8.30-11.30pm Sun-Wed, 1-3.45pm & 8.15pm-midnight Thu-Sat; Ⓜ Sevilla)

Casa Alberto   SPANISH, TAPAS €€

10 Ⓧ Map p54, C4

One of the most atmospheric old *tabernas* (taverns) of Madrid, Casa Alberto has been around since 1827 and occupies a building where Cervantes is said to have written one of his books. The secret to its staying power is vermouth on tap, excellent tapas at the bar and fine sit-down meals. (☑91 429 93 56; www.casaalberto.es; Calle de las Huertas 18; tapas €4-10, raciónes €6.50-16, mains €14-21; ☉restaurant 1.30-4pm & 8pm-midnight Tue-Sat, 1.30-4pm Sun, bar 12.30pm-1.30am Tue-Sat, 12.30-4pm Sun, closed Sun Jul & Aug; Ⓜ Antón Martín)

Vi Cool   MODERN SPANISH €€

11 Ⓧ Map p54, B4

Catalan master chef Sergi Arola is one of the most restless and relentlessly creative culinary talents in the country. Aside from his showpiece **Sergi Arola Gastro** (☑91 310 21 69; www. sergiarola.es; Calle de Zurbano 31; mains €49-58, set menus €49-195; ☉2-3.30pm & 9-11.30pm Tue-Sat Sep-May; Ⓜ Alonso Martínez), he has dabbled in numerous new restaurants around the capital and in Barcelona, and this is one of his most interesting yet. (☑91 429 49 13; www.vi-cool.com; Calle de las Huertas 12; mains €8-19; ☉1.30-4.15pm & 8.30pm-12.15am Tue-Sun; Ⓜ Antón Martín)

Ramiro's Tapas Wine Bar

TAPAS €€

12 🍴 Map p54, C4

One of the best tapas bars to open in Madrid in recent years, this fine gastrobar offers up traditional tapas with subtle but original touches. Most of the cooking comes from Castilla y León but they do exceptional things with cured meats and prawns. Highly recommended. (📞91 843 73 47; Calle de Atocha 51; tapas from €4.50, raciónes from €10; ⏱1-4.30pm & 8-11.30pm Mon-Sat, 1-4.30pm Sun; Ⓜ Antón Martín)

Los Gatos

TAPAS €€

13 🍴 Map p54, D4

Tapas you can point to without deciphering the menu and eclectic old-world decor (from bullfighting memorabilia to a fresco of skeletons at the bar) make this a popular choice down the bottom end of Huertas. The most popular orders are the *canapés* (tapas on toast), which, we have to say, are rather delicious. (📞91 429 30 67; Calle de Jesús 2; tapas from €3.50; ⏱11am-2am; Ⓜ Antón Martín)

La Huerta de Tudela

NAVARRAN €€

14 🍴 Map p54, C4

A bastion of fine cooking from the northern Spanish region of Navarra, La Huerta de Tudela and its chef Ricardo Gil do excellent seasonal vegetable dishes, as well as some excellent steaks and stews. The fantastic range of set menus includes one for coeliacs and another for vegetarians and vegans – typical of the thought that goes into this place. (📞91 420 44 18; www.lahuertadetudela.com; Calle del Prado 15; mains €14-22, set menus €36-44; ⏱1.30-4pm & 8.30-11.30pm Mon-Sat, 1.30-3.30pm Sun; Ⓜ Antón Martín)

La Terraza del Casino

MODERN SPANISH €€€

15 🍴 Map p54, C2

Perched atop the lavish Casino de Madrid building, this temple of haute cuisine is presided over by celebrity chef Paco Roncero and is the proud bearer of two Michelin stars. It's all about culinary experimentation, with a menu that changes as each new idea emerges from the laboratory and moves into the kitchen. The *menú de degustación* (€135) is a fabulous avalanche of tastes. (📞91 532 12 75; www.casinodemadrid.es; Calle de Alcalá 15; mains €35-45, lunch set menu €69; ⏱1-4pm & 9pm-midnight Mon-Sat; Ⓜ Sevilla)

Lhardy

SPANISH €€€

16 🍴 Map p54, B3

This Madrid landmark (since 1839) is an elegant treasure trove of takeaway gourmet tapas downstairs, while the six upstairs dining areas are the upmarket preserve of traditional Madrid dishes with an occasional hint of French influence. House specialities include *cocido a la madrileña* (meat-and-chickpea stew; €36), and pheasant and wild duck in an orange perfume. (📞91 521 33 85; www.lhardy.com; Carrera de San Jerónimo 8; mains €19-38; ⏱1-3.30pm & 8.30-11pm Mon-Sat, 1-3.30pm Sun, closed Aug; Ⓜ Sol, Sevilla)

La Terraza del Casino

Sidrería Vasca Zeraín

BASQUE €€€

17 Map p54, D4

In the heart of the Barrio de las Letras, this sophisticated restaurant is one of the best places in town to sample Basque cuisine. The essential staples include cider, *bacalao* and wonderful steaks, while there are also a few splashes of creativity thrown in (the secret's in the sauce). We highly recommend the *menú sidrería* (cider-house menu; €36.30). (☏91 429 79 09; www.restaurante-vasco-zerain-sidreria.es; Calle Quevedo 3; mains €14-38; ☺1.30-4pm & 7.30pm-midnight Mon-Sat, 1.30-4pm Sun, closed Aug; Ⓜ Antón Martín)

Drinking

La Venencia

BAR

18 Map p54, C3

La Venencia is a *barrio* classic, with fine sherry from Sanlúcar and *manzanilla* (dry sherry) from Jeréz poured straight from the dusty wooden barrels, accompanied by a small selection of tapas with an Andalucian bent. Otherwise, there's no music, no flashy decorations; it's all about you, your *fino* (sherry) and your friends. As one reviewer put it, it's 'a classic among classics'. (☏91 429 73 13; Calle de Echegaray 7; ☺12.30-3.30pm & 7.30pm-1.30am; Ⓜ Sol, Sevilla)

El Imperfecto

COCKTAIL BAR

19 📍 Map p54, C4

Its name notwithstanding, the 'Imperfect One' is our ideal Huertas bar, with occasional live jazz and a drinks menu as long as a saxophone, ranging from cocktails (€7, or two mojitos for €10) and spirits to milkshakes, teas and creative coffees. Its pina colada is one of the best we've tasted and the atmosphere is agreeably buzzy yet chilled. (Plaza de Matute 2; ⏰5pm-2.30am Mon-Thu, 3pm-2.30am Fri & Sat; Ⓜ Antón Martín)

La Terraza del Urban

COCKTAIL BAR

20 📍 Map p54, C3

A strong contender with The Roof and **Splash Óscar** (La Terraza de Arriba; Plaza de Vázquez de Mella 12; ⏰6.30pm-2.30am Wed & Thu, 4.30pm-2.30am Fri-Sun mid-May–mid-Sep; Ⓜ Gran Vía) for the prize for best rooftop bar in Madrid,

this indulgent terrace sits atop the five-star Urban Hotel and has five-star views with five-star prices. Worth every euro, but it's only open while the weather's warm, usually from sometime in May to late-ish September. (📞91 787 77 70; Carrera de San Jerónimo 34; ⏰noon-8pm Sun & Mon, noon-3am Tue-Sat mid-May–Sep; Ⓜ Sevilla)

Taberna Alhambra

BAR

21 📍 Map p54, B3

There can be a certain sameness about the bars between Sol and Huertas, which is why this fine old *taberna* stands out. The striking facade and exquisite tile work of the interior are quite beautiful; however, this place is anything but stuffy and the feel is cool, casual and busy. They serve tapas and, later at night, there are some fine flamenco tunes. (📞91 521 07 08; Calle de la Victoria 9; ⏰11am-1.30am Sun-Wed, 11am-2am Thu, 11am-2.30am Fri & Sat; Ⓜ Sol)

Dos Gardenias

BAR

22 📍 Map p54, D4

When Huertas starts to overwhelm, this tranquil little bar is the perfect antidote. The flamenco and chill-out music ensure a relaxed vibe, while sofas, softly lit colours and some of the best mojitos (and exotic teas) in the *barrio* make this the perfect spot to ease yourself into or out of the night. (📞627 003571; Calle de Santa María 13; ⏰9.30pm-2.30am Tue-Sat; Ⓜ Antón Martín)

Q Local Life

La Mallorquina

Right on Sol, **La Mallorquina** (📞91 521 12 01; www.pastelerialamallorquina. es; Plaza de la Puerta del Sol 8; pastries from €2; ⏰9am-9.15pm; Ⓜ Sol) is a classic pastry shop that's packed to the rafters by locals who just couldn't pass by without stopping. The most popular order is an *ensaimada* (a light pastry dusted with icing sugar) from Mallorca.

Understand

Pedro Almodóvar

La Movida Madrileña

Born in a small, impoverished village in Castilla-La Mancha, Almodóvar once remarked that in such conservative rural surrounds, 'I felt as if I'd fallen from another planet.' After he moved to Madrid in 1969 he found his spiritual home and began his career making underground Super-8 movies and making a living by selling secondhand goods at El Rastro flea market. His early films *Pepi, Luci, Bom y otras chicas del montón* (Pepi, Luci, Bom and the Other Girls; 1980) and *Laberinto de pasiones* (Labyrinth of Passions; 1982) – the film that brought a young Antonio Banderas to attention – announced him as the icon of *la movida madrileña*, the explosion of hedonism and creativity in the early years of post-Franco Spain. Almodóvar had both in bucketloads; he peppered his films with candy-bright colours and characters leading lives where sex and drugs were the norm. By night Almodóvar performed in Madrid's most famous *movida* bars as part of a drag act called Almodóvar & McNamara. He even appeared in this latter role in *Laberinto de pasiones*.

Later Work

By the mid-1980s *madrileños* had adopted him as one of the city's most famous sons and he went on to broaden his fanbase with quirkily comic looks at modern Spain, generally set in the capital, such as *Mujeres al borde de un ataque de nervios* (Women on the Verge of a Nervous Breakdown; 1988) and *¡Átame!* (Tie Me Up! Tie Me Down!; 1990). *Todo sobre mi madre* (All About My Mother; 1999) won Almodóvar his first Oscar for Best Foreign Film and is also notable for the coming of age of the Madrid-born actress Penélope Cruz, who had starred in a number of Almodóvar films and was considered part of a select group of the director's leading ladies long before she became a Hollywood star. Other outstanding movies in a formidable portfolio include *Tacones lejanos* (High Heels; 1991) in which Villa Rosa (p62) makes an appearance; *Hable con ella* (Talk to Her; 2002), for which he won a Best Original Screenplay Oscar; and *Volver* (Return; 2006), which reunited Almodóvar with Penélope Cruz to popular and critical acclaim.

Entertainment

Café Central   JAZZ

23 ⭐ Map p54, B4

In 2011 the respected jazz magazine *Down Beat* included this art deco bar on the list of the world's best jazz clubs, the only place in Spain to earn the prestigious accolade (said by some to be the jazz equivalent of earning a Michelin star). With well over 9000 gigs under its belt, it rarely misses a beat. (☑91 369 41 43; www.cafecentralmadrid.com; Plaza del Ángel 10; admission €12-18; ⏱12.30pm-2.30am Sun-Thu, 12.30pm-3.30am Fri & Sat, performances 9pm; Ⓜ Antón Martín, Sol)

Ⓠ Local Life

Calle de la Paz & Around

Just behind Plaza del la Puerta del Sol, Calle de la Paz has a quirky collection of shops that point to some peculiarly local pursuits. Where Calle del Correos meets Plaza de Pontejos is **Almacén de Pontejos** (☑91 521 55 94; www.almacendepontejos.com; Plaza de Pontejos 2; ⏱9.30am-2pm & 4.30-8.15pm Mon-Fri, 9.30am-2pm Sat; Ⓜ Sol), one of numerous places selling fabrics, buttons, and all manner of knicks and knacks for dressmakers – it's an intriguing hidden subculture, and these shops can throng with people. Nearby Santarrufina is a gilded outpost of Spanish Catholicism in all its excess.

Teatro de la Zarzuela   THEATRE

24 ⭐ Map p54, D3

This theatre, built in 1856, is the premier place to see *zarzuela* (a Spanish mix of theatre, music and dance). It also hosts a smattering of classical music and opera, as well as the cutting edge Compañía Nacional de Danza. (☑91 524 54 00; teatrodelazarzuela.mcu.es; Calle de Jovellanos 4; tickets €5-50; ⏱box office noon-6pm Mon-Fri, 3-6pm Sat & Sun; Ⓜ Banco de España, Sevilla)

Sala El Sol   LIVE MUSIC

25 ⭐ Map p54, B2

Madrid institutions don't come any more beloved than Sala El Sol. It opened in 1979, just in time for *la movida madrileña* (the Madrid scene), and quickly established itself as a leading stage for all the icons of the era, such as Nacha Pop and Alaska y los Pegamoides. (☑91 532 64 90; www.elsolmad.com; Calle de los Jardines 3; ⏱midnight-5.30am Tue-Sat Jul-Sep; Ⓜ Gran Vía)

Villa Rosa   FLAMENCO

26 ⭐ Map p54, B4

Villa Rosa has been going strong since 1914 and has seen many manifestations – it made its name as a flamenco venue and has recently returned to its roots with well-priced shows and meals that won't break the bank. (☑91 521 36 89; www.tablaoflamencovillarosa.com; Plaza de Santa Ana 15; show & drink adult/child from €32/17; ⏱11pm-6am Mon-Sat, shows 8.30pm &

10.45pm Sun-Thu, 8.30pm, 10.45pm &
12.15am Fri & Sat; Ⓜ Sol)

Costello Café & Niteclub

LIVE MUSIC

27 ☆ Map p54, B2

Very cool. Costello Café & Niteclub
weds smooth-as-silk ambience to
an innovative mix of pop, rock and
fusion in Warholesque surrounds.
There's live music (pop and rock,
often of the indie variety) at 9.30pm
every night except Sundays, with
resident and visiting DJs keeping
you on your feet until closing time
from Thursday to Saturday. (☎ 91
522 18 15; www.costelloclub.com; Calle del
Caballero de Gracia 10; admission €5-10;
☺ 8pm-3am Sun-Wed, 6pm-3.30am Thu-Sat;
Ⓜ Gran Vía)

Shopping

Casa de Diego

ACCESSORIES

28 🔒 Map p54, B3

This classic shop has been around
since 1858, making, selling and repair-
ing Spanish fans, shawls, umbrellas
and canes. Service is old style and
occasionally grumpy, but the fans
are works of antique art. There's
another **branch** (☎ 91 531 02 23; Calle del
los Mesoneros Romanos 4; ☺ 9.30am-1.30pm
& 4.45-8pm Mon-Sat; Ⓜ Callao, Sol) nearby.

(www.casadediego.com; Plaza de la Puerta del
Sol 12; ☺ 9.30am-8pm Mon-Sat; Ⓜ Sol)

Santarrufina

RELIGIOUS

29 🔒 Map p54, A3

This gilded outpost of Spanish
Catholicism has to be seen to be
believed. Churches, priests and monasteries are some of the patrons of
this overwhelming three-storey shop
full of everything from simple rosaries
to imposing statues of saints and even
a litter used to carry the Virgin in pro-
cessions. Head downstairs for a peek
at the extravagant chapel. (☎ 91 522 23
83; www.santarrufina.com; Calle de la Paz 4;
☺ 10am-2pm & 4.30-8pm Mon-Fri, 10am-2pm
Sat; Ⓜ Sol)

María Cabello

WINE

30 🔒 Map p54, C4

All wine shops should be like this.
This family-run corner shop really
knows its wines and the interior has
scarcely changed since 1913, with
wooden shelves and even a faded
ceiling fresco. There are fine wines
in abundance (mostly Spanish, and a
few foreign bottles), with some 500
labels on show or tucked away out the
back. (☎ 91 429 60 88; Calle de Echegaray
19; ☺ 9.30am-2.30pm & 5.30-9pm Mon-Fri,
10am-2.30pm & 6.30-9.30pm Sat; Ⓜ Sevilla,
Antón Martín)

Explore

El Retiro & the Art Museums

Madrid's golden mile of art takes in three of Europe's most prestigious and rewarding art galleries, nicely carving up centuries of European art between them. Galleries aside, the Paseo del Prado is a gracious tree-lined boulevard of singular beauty, lined with museums and gardens. Away to the east, the Parque del Buen Retiro is one of our favourite places in the city.

The Sights in a Day

☼ Get to the **Museo del Prado** (p66) for opening time to avoid the crowds; spend at least two hours in the museum, more if you don't plan to return on another day. When you finally tear yourself away, rest in the **Real Jardín Botánico** (p136), before lunching on some of Madrid's most innovative tapas at **Estado Puro** (p83).

☼ It would be overkill to attempt all three of the major galleries in a single day, so choose between the broad journey through European art at **Museo Thyssen-Bornemisza** (p76) and the contemporary art, including Picasso's *Guernica*, at **Centro de Arte Reina Sofía** (p72). After a couple of hours at the gallery of your choice, visit the **Iglesia de San Jerónimo El Real** (p71) and **Plaza de la Cibeles** (p83) en route to the **Parque del Buen Retiro** (p80) – spend as much time wandering through these glorious gardens as you can.

☾ After dinner at **Viridiana** (p83), **Kapital** (p83) is your only option for nightlife, although it often doesn't open until midnight. Fortunately it's worth waiting for and the bars of Huertas are right next door to help you fill in the time.

⊙ Top Sights

Museo del Prado (p66)

Centro de Arte Reina Sofía (p72)

Museo Thyssen-Bornemisza (p76)

Parque del Buen Retiro (p80)

♥ Best of El Retiro & the Art Museums

Old Spanish Masters
Goya (p67)

Velázquez (p69)

Zurbarán (p69)

Modern Spanish Masters
Picasso (p73)

Dalí (p74)

Miró (p73)

Chillida (p74)

Barceló (p74)

The Best of the Rest
Bosch (p70)

Caravaggio (p77)

Van Gogh (p77)

Getting There

Ⓜ **Metro** The main stations for the Paseo del Prado and the art museums are, at the northern end, Banco de España station (line 2), and at the southern end, Atocha station (line 1).

Top Sights
Museo del Prado

Welcome to one of the world's premier art galleries. The more than 7000 paintings held in the Museo del Prado's collection (although only around 1500 are on display at any one time) are like a window into the historical vagaries of the Spanish soul, at once grand and imperious in the royal paintings of Velázquez, darkly tumultuous in Goya's *Pinturas Negras* (Black Paintings) and outward-looking with sophisticated works of art from all across Europe.

◉ Map p82, B3

www.museodelprado.es

Paseo del Prado

adult/child €14/free, free 6-8pm Mon-Sat, 5-7pm Sun, audioguides €3.50

⊙10am-8pm Mon-Sat, 10am-7pm Sun

Ⓜ Banco de España

Don't Miss

El Dos de Mayo (Goya)
Goya is on all three floors of the Prado, but begin at the southern end of the ground or lower level. In rooms 64 and 65, Goya's *El dos de mayo* and *El tres de mayo* rank among Madrid's most emblematic paintings; they bring to life the 1808 anti-French revolt and subsequent execution of insurgents in Madrid.

Pinturas Negras (Goya)
In rooms 66 and 67, Goya's disturbing Black Paintings are so named for the distorted animalesque appearance of their characters. The *Saturno devorando a su hijo* (Saturn Devouring His Son) evokes a writhing mass of tortured humanity, while *La romería de San Isidro* and *Aquelarre (el gran cabrón)* are dominated by the compelling individual faces of the condemned souls.

El Coloso
An interesting footnote to *Pinturas Negras* is *El coloso*, a Goyaesque work that was long considered part of the master's portfolio until the Prado's experts decided otherwise in 2008. The painting and its story are found adjacent to the Black Paintings.

La Família de Carlos IV (Goya)
This painting is a small fragment of Spanish history transferred to canvas. It shows the royal family in 1800 with Fernando (later Fernando VII) dressed in blue on the left. His fiancée has not yet been chosen, which may be why Goya depicts her with no facial definition. Goya portrayed himself in the background just as Velázquez did in *Las meninas*.

☑ Top Tips

▶ Avoid the free opening hours (crowds can really spoil your visit) – first thing in the morning is best.

▶ Despite the various entrances, tickets must be purchased from the ticket office at the building's northern end.

▶ The free plan lists the location of 50 Prado masterpieces and gives room numbers for all major artists.

▶ Plan to make a couple of visits as the Prado can be a little overwhelming if you try to absorb it all at once.

✕ Take a Break

Across the other side of the Paseo del Prado, Estado Puro (p83) is one of Madrid's most exciting tapas bars, with innovative twists on traditional Spanish mainstays.

The cafe inside the Museo del Prado serves reasonable cafeteria-style meals and snacks.

Museo del Prado

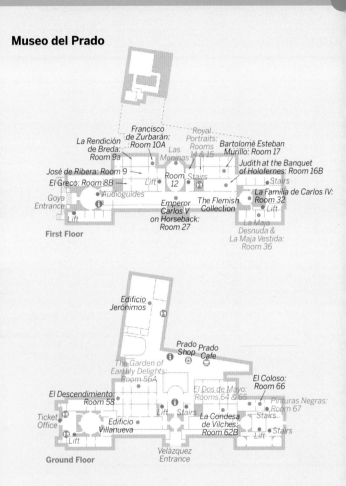

Francisco
de Zurbarán:
Room 10A

Royal
Portraits:
Rooms
14 & 15

Bartolomé Esteban
Murillo: Room 17

La Rendición
de Breda:
Room 9a

Las
Meninas

José de Ribera: Room 9

Judith at the Banquet
of Holofernes: Room 16B

El Greco: Room 8B

Room
12

Stairs

Stairs

Lift

La Familia de Carlos IV:
Room 32

Goya
Entrance

Audioguides

Emperor
Carlos V
on Horseback:
Room 27

The Flemish
Collection

Lift

Lift

La Maja
Desnuda &
La Maja Vestida:
Room 36

First Floor

Edificio
Jerónimos

Prado
Shop

Prado
Cafe

The Garden of
Earthly Delights:
Room 56A

El Coloso:
Room 66

El Descendimiento:
Room 58

El Dos de Mayo:
Rooms 64 & 65

Pinturas Negras:
Room 67

Ticket
Office

Lift

Stairs

Stairs

Edificio
Villanueva

Lift

La Condesa
de Vilches:
Room 62B

Lift

Stairs

Velázquez
Entrance

Ground Floor

More Goya...

On the 1st floor, there are more Goyas. Among them are two more of Goya's best-known and most intriguing oils: *La maja vestida* and *La maja desnuda*. These portraits of an unknown woman, commonly believed to be the Duquesa de Alba (who some think may have been Goya's lover), are identical save for the lack of clothing in the latter.

Las Meninas (Velázquez)

Of all the works by Velázquez, *Las meninas* (Room 12) is what most people come to see. Completed in 1656, it depicts the infant Margarita. The artist portrays himself painting the king and queen, whose images appear, according to some experts, in mirrors behind Velázquez. His mastery of light and colour is never more apparent than here.

Royal Portraits (Velázquez)

The rooms surrounding *Las meninas* (rooms 14 and 15) contain more fine works by Velázquez. Watch in particular for his paintings of various members of royalty who seem to spring off the canvas – Felipe II, Felipe IV, Margarita de Austria (a younger version of whom features in *Las meninas*), El Príncipe Baltasar Carlos and Isabel de Francia – on horseback.

La Rendición de Breda (Velázquez)

Velázquez's masterpiece shows the moment in 1625 in which Spanish general Ambrosio Spinola accepts the surrender of the Dutch town of Breda after a long siege. The Spanish novelist Arturo Pérez-Reverte mixed fantasy and reality in his novel *The Sun Over Breda*, claiming that his character Captain Alatriste appeared in the painting but was later mysteriously erased by Velázquez.

Other Spanish Masters

If Spanish painters have piqued your curiosity, Bartolomé Esteban Murillo, José de Ribera and the stark figures of Francisco de Zurbarán should be on your itinerary. The vivid, almost surreal works by the 16th-century master and adopted Spaniard El Greco, whose figures are characteristically slender and tortured, are also perfectly executed.

La Condesa de Vilches (Madrazo)

The painter was a friend of the model, which may be why he is able to transmit all her grace and sensuality. The light blue dress, the tone of her skin, the brightness in her eyes and her smile suggest a timeless sympathy that endures through the centuries.

The Flemish Collection

The Prado's outstanding collection of Flemish art includes the fulsome figures and bulbous cherubs of Peter Paul Rubens (1577–1640). His signature works are *Las tres gracias* and *Adoración de los reyes magos*. Other fine works in the vicinity include *The Triumph of Death* by Pieter Bruegel and those by Anton Van Dyck.

El Descendimiento
(Van Der Weyden)
This 1435 painting is unusual, both for its size and for the recurring crossbow shapes in the painting's upper corners, which are echoed in the bodies of Mary and Christ (the painting was commissioned by a Crossbow Manufacturers Brotherhood). Once the central part of a triptych, the painting is filled with drama and luminous colours.

The Garden of
Earthly Delights (Bosch)
On no account miss the weird and wonderful *The Garden of Earthly Delights* (Room 56A) by Hieronymus Bosch (c 1450–1516). No one has yet been able to provide a definitive explanation for this hallucinatory work, although many have tried. The closer you look, the harder it is to escape the feeling that he must have been doing some extraordinary drugs.

El Greco
This Greek-born artist (hence the name) is considered the finest of the Prado's Spanish Renaissance painters. Two of his more than 30 paintings in the collection – *The Annunciation* and *The Flight into Egypt* – were painted in Italy before the artist arrived in Spain, while *The Trinity* and *Knight with His Hand on his Breast* are considered his most important works.

Judith at the Banquet of
Holofernes (Rembrandt)
The only painting by Rembrandt in the Prado's collection was completed

Understand
The Life & Times of Goya

Francisco José de Goya y Lucientes (1746–1828) started his career as a cartoonist in Madrid's Royal Tapestry Workshop. In 1792, illness left him deaf; many critics speculate that his condition was largely responsible for his wild, often merciless style that would become increasingly unshackled from convention. By 1799 Goya was appointed Carlos IV's court painter.

After painting his enigmatic masterpieces *La maja vestida* and *La maja desnuda*, and the frescoes in Madrid's Ermita de San Antonio de la Florida, the arrival of the French and war in 1808 had a profound impact on Goya; *El dos de mayo* and, more dramatically, *El tres de mayo* are unforgiving portrayals of the brutality of war.

After he retired to the Quinta del Sordo (Deaf Man's House), west of the Río Manzanares in Madrid, he created his nightmarish *Pinturas Negras* (Black Paintings). Executed on the walls of the house, they were later removed and now hang in the Prado. Goya spent the last years of his life in voluntary exile in France, where he continued to paint until his death.

in 1634; note the artist's signature and date on the arm of the chair. The painting shows a master at the peak of his powers, with a masterly use of the chiaroscuro style, and the astonishing detail in the subject's clothing and face.

Emperor Carlos V on Horseback (Titian)

Considered one of the finest equestrian and royal portraits in art history, this 16th-century work is said to be the forerunner to similar paintings by Velázquez a century later. One of the great masters of the Renaissance, Titian (1488–1576) was entering his most celebrated period as a painter when he created this, and it is widely recognised as one of his masterpieces.

The Best of the Rest...

No matter how long you spend in the Prado, there's always more to discover, such as the paintings by Dürer, Rafael, Tintoretto, Sorolla, Gainsborough, Fra Angelico, Tiepolo...

Edificio Villanueva

The western wing (Edificio Villanueva) was completed in 1785 as the neoclassical Palacio de Villanueva. It served as a cavalry barracks for Napoleon's troops between 1808 and 1813. In 1814 King Fernando VII decided to use the palace as a museum. Five years later the Museo del Prado opened with 311 Spanish paintings on display.

Edificio Jerónimos

The Prado's eastern wing (Edificio Jerónimos) is part of the Prado's stunning modern extension. Dedicated to temporary exhibitions (usually to display Prado masterpieces held in storage for decades for lack of wall space), its main attraction is the 2nd-floor cloisters. Built in 1672 with local granite, the cloisters were, until recently, attached to the adjacent Iglesia de San Jerónimo El Real.

Casón del Buen Retiro

This building overlooking the Parque del Buen Retiro is run as an academic library by the nearby Museo del Prado. The Prado runs guided visits to the stunning Hall of the Ambassadors, which is crowned by the astonishing 1697 ceiling fresco *The Apotheosis of the Spanish Monarchy* by Luca Giordano.

Iglesia de San Jerónimo El Real

Tucked away behind the Museo del Prado, this **chapel** (📞91 420 35 78; Calle de Ruiz de Alarcón; ⏲10am-1pm & 5-8.30pm Mon-Sat Oct-Jun, hours vary Jul-Sep; Ⓜ Atocha, Banco de España) was traditionally favoured by the Spanish royal family, and King Juan Carlos I was crowned here in 1975 upon the death of Franco. The sometimes-sober, sometimes-splendid mock-Isabelline interior is actually a 19th-century reconstruction. What remained of the former cloisters has been incorporated into the Museo del Prado.

Top Sights
Centro de Arte Reina Sofía

Home to Picasso's *Guernica*, arguably Spain's single-most famous artwork, and a host of other important Spanish artists, the Centro de Arte Reina Sofía is Madrid's premier collection of contemporary art. In addition to plenty of paintings by Picasso, other major drawcards are works by Salvador Dalí and Joan Miró. The collection principally spans the 20th century up to the 1980s, and although the occasional non-Spanish artist makes an appearance, most of the collection is strictly peninsular.

👁 Map p82, A5

www.museoreinasofia.es
Calle de Santa Isabel 52

adult/concession €8/free, free 1.30-7pm Sun, 7-9pm Mon & Wed-Sat

🕙10am-9pm Mon & Wed-Sat, 10am-7pm Sun

Ⓜ Atocha

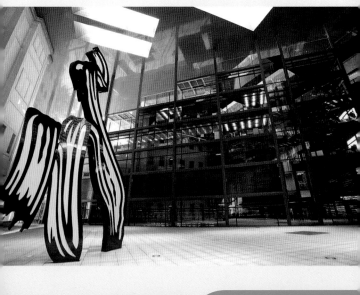

Don't Miss

Guernica (Picasso)

Claimed by some to be the single-most important artwork of the 20th century, Pablo Picasso's *Guernica* is an icon of the cubist style for which Picasso became famous. You could easily spend hours studying the painting, but take the time to both examine the detail of its various constituent elements and step back to get an overview of this extraordinary canvas.

Preparatory Sketches

To deepen your understanding of *Guernica*, don't neglect the sketches that Picasso painted as he prepared to execute his masterpiece. They're found in the rooms surrounding Room 206 (allowing you to move between and compare the sketches and main painting with ease). They offer an intriguing insight into the development of this seminal work.

Other Cubist Masters

Picasso may have been the driving force behind the cubist form, but he was soon joined by others who saw its potential. Picasso is said to have been influenced by the mask traditions of Africa, and these elements can also be discerned in the work of Madrid-born Juan Gris (1887–1927) and Georges Braque (1882–1963), two of the undoubted masters of the genre.

Joan Miró

The work of Joan Miró (1893–1983) is defined by often delightfully bright primary colours. Since his paintings became a symbol of the Barcelona Olympics in 1992, his work has begun to receive the international acclaim it so richly deserves. The museum is a fine place to get a representative sample of his innovative work.

☑ Top Tips

▶ The permanent collection is on the 2nd and 4th floors of the museum's main wing, the Edificio Sabatini.

▶ *Guernica*'s location (Room 206, 2nd floor) never changes.

▶ The Reina Sofía's paintings are grouped together by theme rather than artist – pick up a copy of the *Planos de Museo* (Museum Floorplans).

▶ The museum's *Guide to the Collection* (€22), available from the gift shop, takes a closer look at 80 of the museum's signature works.

✖ Take a Break

Visible from the museum's entrance, **El Brillante** (☎91 528 69 66; Plaza del Emperador Carlos V; bocadillos €4.50-7, raciónes €7.50-12; ⏱7.30am-2.30am Sep-Jul; Ⓜ Atocha) is a breezy, no-frills bar-eatery. It's a Madrid institution for its *bocadillos* (filled rolls) and *chocolate con churros*.

Salvador Dalí

The Reina Sofía is also home to around 20 canvases by Salvador Dalí (1904–89), of which the most famous is perhaps the surrealist extravaganza *El gran masturbador* (1929); at once disturbing and utterly compelling, this is one of the museum's stand-out paintings. Look also for a strange bust of a certain Joelle done by Dalí and his friend Man Ray.

More Surrealism

Dalí aside, the Reina Sofía doesn't have many surrealist paintings, but just as lesser-known masters of the cubist style provide a reference point for Picasso, so Max Ernst (1891–1976) provides an intriguing counterpoint to Dalí. His sculpture *La bella alemana* (1934–35) is typical of his style.

Contemporary Spanish Artists I

If you can tear yourself away from the big names, the Reina Sofía offers a terrific opportunity to learn more about lesser-known 20th-century Spanish artists. Among these are: Miquel Barceló (b 1957); *madrileño* artist José Gutiérrez Solana (1886–1945); the renowned Basque painter Ignazio Zuloaga (1870–1945); and Benjamín Palencia (1894–1980), whose paintings capture the turbulence of Spain in the 1930s.

Contemporary Spanish Artists II

The late Barcelona painter Antoni Tàpies (1923–2012), for years one of Spain's most creative and extraordinary talents, is represented, as is the pop art of Eduardo Arroyo (b 1937),

abstract painters such as Eusebio Sempere (1923–85) and members of the Equipo 57 group (founded in 1957 by a group of Spanish artists in exile in Paris), including Pablo Palazuelo (1916–2007).

Lorca

As always, Federico García Lorca (1898–1936) belongs in a class of his own. Although better known as a poet and playwright, he is represented in the Reina Sofía by a number of his sketches.

Sculptures

Of the sculptors, watch in particular for Pablo Gargallo (1881–1934), whose work in bronze includes a bust of Picasso, and the renowned Basque sculptors Jorge Oteiza (1908–2003) and Eduardo Chillida (1924–2002). Chillida's sculptures, rendered in rusted wrought-iron, are among Spanish art's most intriguing (and pleasing) forms.

Architecture

Beyond its artwork, the Reina Sofía is an important architectural landmark, adapted from the shell of an 18th-century hospital with eye-catching external glass lifts. The stunning extension (the Edificio Nouvel) that spreads along the western tip of the Plaza del Emperador Carlos V, hosts temporary exhibitions, auditoriums, the bookshop, a cafe and the museum's library.

Understand

Picasso's Guernica

Guernica is one of the most famous paintings in the world, a signature work of cubism whose disfiguration of the human form would become an eloquent symbol of a world's outrage at the horrors wrought upon the innocent by modern warfare. For some it's an overtly political work, a moment captured in time when the world lost its innocence. For others it is the painting that announced the arrival of an entirely new genre, of which it remains the most enduring symbol.

After the Spanish Civil War broke out in 1936, Picasso was commissioned by the Republican government of Madrid to do the painting for the Paris Exposition Universelle in 1937. As news filtered out about the bombing of Gernika (Guernica) in the Basque Country by Hitler's Legión Condor at the request of Franco, Picasso committed his anger to canvas. At least 200 people (possibly many more) died in the 26 April 1937 attack and much of the town was destroyed. To understand the painting's earth-shattering impact at the time, it must be remembered that the attack on Guernica represented the first use of airborne military hardware to devastating effect, and served as a precursor to the devastation wrought by weapons of mass destruction in WWII.

Guernica has always been a controversial work and was initially derided by many as being more propaganda than art – Picasso was no friend of Franco's and he would spend much of his later life in exile. The 3.5m by 7.8m painting subsequently migrated to the USA, where it spent time in numerous museums across the country. It only returned to Spain in 1981, in keeping with Picasso's wish that the painting return to Spanish shores only once democracy had been restored.

Given the subject matter, the Basques believe that its true home is in the Basque Country and calls to have it moved there continue unabated. Such a move is, however, unlikely to happen any time soon, with the Reina Sofía arguing that the painting is too fragile to be moved again.

Top Sights
Museo Thyssen-Bornemisza

One of the most extraordinary private collections of predominantly European art in the world, the Museo Thyssen-Bornemisza is a worthy member of Madrid's 'Golden Triangle' of art. Where the Museo del Prado or Centro de Arte Reina Sofía enable you to study the body of work of a particular artist in depth, the Thyssen is a place to immerse yourself in a breathtaking breadth of artistic styles. Not surprisingly, it often ends up being many visitors' favourite Madrid art gallery.

◉ Map p82, A2

www.museothyssen.org

Paseo del Prado 8

adult/child €10/free, free Mon

🕐 10am-7pm Tue-Sun, noon-4pm Mon

Ⓜ Banco de España

Don't Miss

Religious Art

The 2nd floor, which is home to medieval art, includes some real gems hidden among the mostly 13th- and 14th-century and predominantly Italian, German and Flemish religious paintings and triptychs. Much of it is sacred art that won't appeal to everyone, but it somehow captures the essence of medieval Europe.

Rooms 5 & 10

Unless you've a specialist's eye for the paintings that fill the first four rooms, pause for the first time in Room 5 where you'll find one work by Italy's Piero della Francesca (1410–92) and the instantly recognisable *Portrait of King Henry VIII* by Holbein the Younger (1497–1543), before continuing on to Room 10 for the evocative 1586 *Massacre of the Innocents* by Lucas Van Valckenborch.

Spain & Venice

Room 11 is dedicated to El Greco (with three pieces) and his Venetian contemporaries Tintoretto and Titian, while Caravaggio and the Spaniard José de Ribera dominate Room 12. A single painting each by Murillo and Zurbarán add further Spanish flavour in the two rooms that follow, while the exceptionally rendered views of Venice by Canaletto (1697–1768) should on no account be missed.

European Masters

Best of all, on the top floor is the extension (Rooms A to H), which houses the collection of Carmen Thyssen-Bornemisza; the rest belonged to her late husband, Baron Thyssen-Bornemisza, a German-Hungarian magnate. Room C houses paintings by Canaletto, Constable and Van Gogh, while the stunning Room H includes works by Monet, Sisley, Renoir, Pissarro and Degas.

☑ Top Tips

▶ Don't come here expecting many paintings from a single master, but instead expect single paintings from many masters.

▶ The collection's oldest works are on the top floor, with contemporary art on the ground floor. For a journey through the history of art, start on the 2nd floor and work your way down.

▶ The excellent audioguide allows you to zero in on particular paintings, which counters the feeling of being overwhelmed by such a wide-ranging collection.

✗ Take a Break

Estado Puro (p83), just around the roundabout within sight of the museum entrance, is sophisticated and a relentlessly creative tapas bar.

For something a little more earthy and eclectic, Los Gatos (p58) also does tapas but with a more traditional slant.

Museo Thyssen-Bornemizsa

Second Floor

European Masters: Rooms A to H

Flemish Masters: Rooms 19 to 21

Caravaggio & José de Ribera: Room 12

Massacre of the Innocents

Portrait of King Henry VIII

El Greco, Tintoretto & Titian: Room 11

First Floor

Baroness Collection: Rooms I to P

Goya: Room 31

Gainsborough: Room 28

Picasso, Matisse, Cézanne, Gauguin, Munch: Rooms 33 to 35

Van Gogh, Manet, Monet, Pisarro & Renoir: Room 32

Ground Floor

Audioguides

Contemporary Icons: Rooms 46 to 48

Ticket Office

Cubism & Surrealism: Rooms 41 to 44

Shop

Chagall & Dalí: Room 45

Dutch & Flemish Masters

Before heading downstairs to the 1st floor, a detour to Rooms 19 through to 21 will satisfy those devoted to 17th-century Dutch and Flemish masters, Anton Van Dyck, Jan Brueghel the Elder, Rubens and Rembrandt (one painting).

Gainsborough & Goya

If all that sounds impressive, the 1st floor is where the Thyssen really shines. There's a Gainsborough in Room 28 and a Goya in Room 31, but even these are considered secondary to what's around the corner.

Room 32

If you've been skimming the surface, Room 32 is the place to linger over every painting. Van Gogh's astonishingly textured *Les Vessenots* is a masterpiece, and the same applies to Manet's *Woman in Riding Habit*, Monet's *The Thaw at Véthueil*, Renoir's *Woman with a Parasol in a Garden*, and Pissarro's *Rue Saint-Honoré in the Afternoon*. Simply extraordinary.

Rooms 33 to 35

There's no time to catch your breath, because Room 33 is similarly something special with Cézanne, Toulouse-Lautrec, Gauguin, and Degas all on show. The big names continue in Room 34 (Picasso, Matisse and Modigliani) and 35 (Edvard Munch and Egon Schiele).

The Baroness Collection

In the 1st floor's extension (Rooms I to P), Room K has works by Monet, Pissaro, Sorolla and Sisley, while Room L is the domain of Gauguin (including his iconic *Mata Mua*), Degas and Toulouse-Lautrec. Rooms M (Munch), N (Kandinsky), O (Matisse and Georges Braque) and P (Picasso, Matisse, Edward Hopper and Juan Gris) round out an outrageously rich journey.

Cubism & Surrealism

Down on the ground floor, in Room 41 you'll see a nice mix of the big three of cubism, Picasso, Georges Braque and Madrid's own Juan Gris, along with several other contemporaries. Kandinsky is the main drawcard in Room 43, while there's an early Salvador Dalí alongside Max Ernst and Paul Klee in Room 44.

Room 45

Picasso appears again in Room 45, another one of the gallery's stand-out rooms; its treasures include works by Marc Chagall and Dalí's hallucinatory *Dream Caused by the Flight of a Bee Around a Pomegranate a Second Before Waking Up*.

Contemporary Icons

There's no let-up as the Thyssen builds to a stirring climax. Room 46 has Joan Miró's *Catalan Peasant with a Guitar*, Jackson Pollock's *Brown and Silver I* and the deceptively simple but strangely pleasing *Green on Maroon* by Mark Rothko. In Rooms 47 and 48, Francis Bacon, Roy Lichtenstein, Henry Moore and Lucian Freud, Sigmund's Berlin-born grandson, are all represented.

Top Sights
Parque del Buen Retiro

The glorious gardens of El Retiro are as beautiful as any you'll find in a European city. Laid out in the 17th century by Felipe IV as the preserve of kings, queens and their intimates, the park was opened to the public in 1868 – ever since, it's been a favourite haunt of *madrileños*. Dotted with marble monuments, landscaped lawns, the occasional elegant building and abundant greenery, it's quiet and contemplative during the week, but comes to life on weekends.

⊙ Map p82, C2

⊙6am-midnight May-Sep, to 11pm Oct-Apr

Ⓜ Retiro, Príncipe de Vergara, Ibiza, Atocha

Palacio de Cristal

Don't Miss

Lake (Estanque)

An El Retiro focal point, the artificial lake (*estanque*) is watched over by the massive, ornamental **Monument to Alfonso XII**, complete with marble lions. Renting a **row boat** (per boat per 45min weekdays/weekends €5.80/7.50; ⏱10am-8.30pm Apr-Sep, to 5.45pm Oct-Mar) is a very Madrid thing to do.

Palacio de Cristal

Hidden among the trees south of the lake, the **Palacio de Cristal** (📞91 574 66 14; www.museoreinasofia.es; ⏱10am-10pm Apr-Sep, 10am-6pm Oct-Mar; Ⓜ Retiro) is a magnificent metal-and-glass pavilion, arguably El Retiro's most beautiful architectural monument. Built in 1887 as a winter garden for exotic flowers, it's now used for temporary exhibitions. Its surrounds are our favourite picnic spot.

Roses & the Devil

At the southern end of the park, near **La Rosaleda** (Rose Garden) with its more than 4000 roses, is a statue of **El Ángel Caído** (the Fallen Angel), one of few statues of the devil anywhere in the world. It sits 666m above sea level...

Madrid's Oldest Tree

Just inside the Puerta de Felipe IV on El Retiro's western side, stands Madrid's oldest tree, a Mexican conifer (*ahuehuete*). Planted in 1633, it was used as a cannon mount by French soldiers during the Napoleonic Wars in the early 19th century.

Romanesque Ruins

In the northeastern corner of the park is the Ermita de San Isidro, one of the few, albeit modest examples of Romanesque architecture in Madrid. Parts of the wall, a side entrance and part of the apse were restored in 1999 and are all that remain of the 13th-century building. When it was built, Madrid was a small village more than 2km away.

☑ Top Tips

▶ If renting a boat on weekends, do so around 3pm to 4pm when most locals are lunching.

▶ Pack a picnic lunch and find an unoccupied stretch of lawn.

▶ Cycling or roller-blading is a terrific way to range far and wide across El Retiro. **Bike & Roll** (📞91 142 77 93; www.bikeandroll.es; Av de Menéndez Pelayo 2; per hr/day from €4/20; ⏱10am-8pm Mon-Fri, 10am-2pm Sat; 🅿; Ⓜ Príncipe de Vergara) rents both forms of transport and is just off El Retiro's northeastern corner.

✕ Take a Break

Ideal for a picnic lunch, but also a pleasant cafe, Mallorca (p96) is a fine pit-stop en route to or from the park.

Kiosks sell pricey drinks and there are cafes around the park, but little food for sale – another reason we recommend bringing your own.

A | B | C | D

1
Plaza del Rey
Banco de España M
Paseo del Prado M
CENTRO
C de Alcalá
Banco de España M
C de Marqués de Cubas
C de los Madrazo

Paseo de los Recoletos
C de Salustiano
3 Plaza de la Cibeles

JUSTICIA
C de Columela
Retiro M
C de Alcalá

Plaza de la Independencia
Puerta Independencia
Paseo de México

2
C de Zorrilla
Paseo del Prado
Carrera de San Jerónimo

2
Mirador de Madrid
C Valenzuela
C de Montalbán
C de Juan de Mena
Plaza de la Lealtad
C de Antonio Maura

C de Alfonso XII
C de Alfonso XII
5

Paseo de Colombia
Estanque
Puerta Paseo de la Argentina de España RETIRO
Parque del Buen Retiro

Museo Thyssen-Bornemisza

Parque del Buen Retiro
Paseo Parterre

3
C de Cervantes
4
Plaza de Medinaceli
C del Duque
C de Jesús
C de Lope de Vega
HUERTAS
C de las Huertas
C de Moratín

Plaza de Neptuno (Plaza de Cánovas del Castillo)
Museo del Prado

C Felipe IV
C de la Academia
C de Morato
C Casado del Alisal
C Alberto Bosch
C de Espalter

Puerta Felipe IV
Paseo San Pablo
Jerónimos

Paseo de la República de Cuba

Jardín de los Plantales

4
C del Gobernador
C de Fúcar
C de la Alameda
C de Atocha
C de Cenicero

1 Caixa Forum
Real Jardín Botánico

C de Ruiz de Alarcón

Plaza de Bravo Murillo

Puerta Murillo

C de Alfonso XII

Paseo de Fernán Núñez

5
C de Santa Isabel
C Hospital
Centro de Arte Reina Sofía
LAVAPIÉS
C del Doctor Drumén
6
Cuesta de Claudio Moyano
Atocha M
Plaza del Emperador Carlos V
Atocha M
Av de la Ciudad de Barcelona
Paseo de la Infanta Isabel
Atocha Renfe M

N
0   200 m
0   0.1 miles

For reviews see
● Top Sights   p66
● Sights   p83
✕ Eating   p83
🍷 Drinking   p83

Sights

Caixa Forum   MUSEUM, ARCHITECTURE

1 ⊙ Map p82, B4

This extraordinary structure is one of Madrid's most eye-catching landmarks. Seeming to hover above the ground, this brick edifice is topped by an intriguing summit of rusted iron. (☑91 330 73 00; obrasocial.lacaixa.es/nuestroscentros/caixaforummadrid_es.html; Paseo del Prado 36; admission free, exhibitions from €4; ◷10am-8pm; Ⓜ Atocha)

Mirador de Madrid   VIEWPOINT

2 ⊙ Map p82, B1

The views from the summit of the Palacio de Comunicaciones are arguably Madrid's best, sweeping west down over the Plaza de la Cibeles, up the hill towards the sublime Edificio Metrópolis and out to the mountains. (www.centrocentro.org; 8th fl, Palacio de Comunicaciones, Plaza de la Cibeles; adult/child €2/0.50; ◷10.30am-1.30pm & 4-7pm Tue-Sun; Ⓜ Banco de España)

Plaza de la Cibeles   SQUARE

3 ⊙ Map p82, B1

Of all the grand roundabouts that punctuate the Paseo del Prado, Plaza de la Cibeles most evokes the splendour of imperial Madrid. The jewel in the crown is the astonishing **Palacio de Comunicaciones**. The spectacular **fountain of the goddess Cybele** at the centre of the plaza is one of Madrid's most beautiful. (Ⓜ Banco de España)

Eating

Estado Puro   TAPAS €€

4 🍴 Map p82, A3

A slick but casual tapas bar, Estado Puro serves up fantastic tapas, such as the *tortilla española siglo XXI* (21st-century Spanish omelette, served in a glass...), lobster gazpacho and parmesan ice cream. (☑91 330 24 00; www.tapasenestadopuro.com; Plaza Neptuno (Plaza de Cánovas del Castillo) 4; tapas €5-16, mains €13-22; ◷noon-midnight Mon-Sat, noon-4pm Sun; Ⓜ Banco de España, Atocha)

Viridiana   MODERN SPANISH €€€

5 🍴 Map p82, C2

The chef here, Abraham García, is a much-celebrated Madrid figure and his larger-than-life personality is reflected in Viridiana's menu. (☑91 523 44 78; www.restauranteviridiana.com; Calle de Juan de Mena 14; mains €28-38, menú de degustación €100; ◷1.30-4pm & 8pm-midnight; Ⓜ Banco de España)

Drinking

Kapital   CLUB

6 🍷 Map p82, B4

One of the most famous megaclubs in Madrid, this seven-storey venue has something for everyone: from cocktail bars and dance music to karaoke, salsa, hip hop and chilled spaces. Admission from €15. (☑91 420 29 06; www.grupo-kapital.com; Calle de Atocha 125; ◷5.30-10.30pm & midnight-6am Fri & Sat, midnight-6am Thu & Sun; Ⓜ Atocha)

Explore

Salamanca

The *barrio* of Salamanca is Madrid's most exclusive quarter, a place where stately mansions, set back from the street, sit alongside boutiques from the big local and international fashion designers, and where the unmistakeable whiff of old money mingles comfortably with the aspirations of Spain's nouveau riche. Put on your finest clothes and be seen.

The Sights in a Day

☼ Start your morning at the **Museo Lázaro Galdiano** (p86), then follow Calle de Serrano into the heart of Salamanca, pausing en route at the **Museo al Aire Libre** (p92). When you reach Calle de José Ortega y Gasset, one of Europe's great shopping streets, you've arrived at Spain's fashion central. Meander down for lunch at **Restaurante Estay** (p89), **La Colonial de Goya** (p94) or **La Cocina de María Luisa** (p94).

☼ After lunch, shop at **Gallery** (p96), then admire the grand **Biblioteca Nacional** (p92) and stop by the wonderfully renovated **Museo Arqueológico Nacional** (p92). Walk the walk along Calle de Serrano, shopping at **Camper** (p88), **Loewe** (p97), **Agatha Ruiz de la Prada** (p89) and **Manolo Blahnik** (p89), among other icons of Spanish fashion.

☾ Salamanca nights are pretty quiet by Madrid's standards, but there's still plenty to keep you busy. For a pre-dinner drink, join the after-work crowd at **El Lateral** (p89). For one of Madrid's most exciting gastronomic scenes, visit **Platea** (p95). To dance the night away, try **Almonte** (p95) for flamenco tunes.

For a local's day shopping in Salamanca, see p88.

👁 Top Sights
Museo Lázaro Galdiano (p86)

◯ Local Life
Shopping in Upmarket Salamanca (p88)

♥ Best of Salamanca

Spanish Fashion
Agatha Ruiz de la Prada (p89)

Camper (p88)

Loewe (p97)

Manolo Blahnik (p89)

Purificación García (p97)

Gourmet Food Shops
Bombonerías Santa (p89)

Oriol Balaguer (p89)

Mantequería Bravo (p97)

Tapas
Biotza (p94)

La Colonial de Goya (p94)

Restaurante Estay (p89)

Getting There

Ⓜ **Metro** For the heart of Salamanca, Serrano (line 4) and Nuñez de Balboa (5 and 9) stations are best. Useful perimeter stations are Goya (2 and 4), Velázquez (4), Príncipe de Vergara (2 and 9), Retiro (2) and Colón (4).

Top Sights
Museo Lázaro Galdiano

This imposing, early 20th-century Italianate stone mansion set discreetly back from the street was once the home of one Don José Lázaro Galdiano (1862–1947), a successful and cultivated businessman. A quintessential Salamanca personality and patron of culture, he built up an astonishing private art collection that he bequeathed to the city upon his death. It was no mean inheritance, with some 13,000 works of art and objets d'art, a quarter of which are on show at any time.

⊙ Map p90, B2

www.flg.es

Calle de Serrano 122

adult/concession/child €6/3/free, last hour free

🕙 10am-4.30pm Mon & Wed-Sat, 10am-3pm Sun

Ⓜ Gregorio Marañón

Landscape with Smugglers, by Eugenio Lucas Velázquez

Don't Miss

Checklist of Old Masters

It can be difficult to believe the breadth of masterpieces that Señor Lázaro Galdiano gathered during his lifetime, and there's enough here to merit this museum's inclusion among Madrid's best art galleries. The highlights include works by Zurbarán, Claudio Coello, Hieronymus Bosch, Esteban Murillo, El Greco, Lucas Cranach and Constable, and there's even a painting in room 11 attributed to Velázquez.

Goya

As is often the case, Goya belongs in a class of his own. He dominates room 13, while the ceiling of the adjoining room 14 features a collage from some of Goya's more famous works. Some that are easy to recognise include *La maja desnuda*, *La maja vestida* and the frescoes of the Ermita de San Antonio de la Florida

Curio Collection

This remarkable collection ranges beyond paintings to include sculptures, bronzes, miniature figures, jewellery, ceramics, furniture, weapons... clearly he was a man of wide interests. The ground floor is largely given over to a display setting the social context in which Galdiano lived, with hundreds of curios from all around the world on show. There are more on the top floor.

Frescoes & Textiles

The lovely 1st floor, which contains many of the Spanish artworks, is arrayed around the centrepiece of the former ballroom and beneath lavishly frescoed ceilings. And on no account miss the top floor's room 24, which contains some exquisite textiles.

☑ Top Tips

▶ Most museums close on Mondays, but this one bucks the trend by closing Tuesday – don't be caught out.

▶ The museum is a long uphill walk from the rest of Salamanca – take the metro here and walk back down.

▶ Unless you've a specialist interest, the guides on sale at the entrance are unnecessary – English and Spanish labelling is excellent.

▶ Seek out the photos of each room to see how it appeared in Galdiano's prime.

✕ Take a Break

José Luis (p94) is where the young and the wealthy come to sip bottled mineral water and order *tortilla de patatas* (Spanish potato omelette). It's across the road from the museum.

Local Life
Shopping in Upmarket Salamanca

From international designers with no need for introductions to Spanish household names that the shopper in you will adore discovering, Salamanca is a fashionista's dream come true. Add some terrific gourmet food purveyors and casual but classy pit stops along the way and it's a day to remember if shopping gets you excited.

❶ Camper

Spanish fashion is not all haute couture. **Camper** (☎91 578 25 60; www.camper.com; Calle de Serrano 24; ⊙10am-9pm Mon-Sat, noon-8pm Sun; Ⓜ Serrano), the world-famous cool and quirky shoe brand from Mallorca, offers bowling-shoe chic with colourful, fun designs that couple quality with comfort.

❷ Agatha Ruiz de la Prada

Agatha Ruiz de la Prada (☑91 319 05 01; www.agatharuizdelaprada.com; Calle de Serrano 27; ☉10am-8.30pm Mon-Sat; Ⓜ Serrano) has to be seen to be believed, with pinks, yellows and oranges everywhere you turn. It's fun and exuberant, but not just for kids. It also has serious and highly original fashion.

❸ Bombonerías Santa

When locals want a tasteful gift to take to their next dinner party, many of them come to **Bombonerías Santa** (☑91 576 76 25; www.bombonerias-santa.com; Calle de Serrano 56; ☉10am-2pm & 5-8.30pm Mon, 10am-8.30pm Tue-Sat, shorter hours in Jul & Aug; Ⓜ Serrano). The exquisitely presented chocolates here are reason enough to join them, dinner party or not.

❹ Manolo Blahnik

The world-famous shoe designer **Manolo Blahnik** (☑91 575 96 48; www.manoloblahnik.com; Calle de Serrano 58; ☉10am-2pm & 4-8pm Mon-Sat; Ⓜ Serrano) has a boutique along Calle de Serrano. The showroom is exclusive and each shoe is displayed like a work of art.

❺ Restaurante Estay

Backtracking slightly away to the southeast, **Restaurante Estay** (☑91 578 04 70; www.estayrestaurante.com; Calle de Hermosilla 46; tapas €1.75-5, 6-tapas set menu from €13.25; ☉8am-midnight Mon-Thu, 8am-1am Fri & Sat; Ⓜ Velázquez) is partly a Spanish bar, where besuited waiters serve *café con leche*, and also one of the best-loved tapas bars in this part

of town. There's a long list of tapas and it's a classy but casual place to rest before continuing.

❻ Oriol Balaguer

Catalan pastry chef **Oriol Balaguer** (www.oriolbalaguer.com; Calle de José Ortega y Gasset 44; ☉9am-8pm Mon-Fri, 10am-8pm Sat, 10am-2.30pm Sun; Ⓜ Núñez de Balboa) won a prize for the World's Best Dessert (the 'Seven Textures of Chocolate') in 2001. More recently, his croissants won the title of Spain's best in 2014. His chocolate boutique is like a small art gallery dedicated to exquisite, finely crafted chocolate collections and cakes.

❼ Calle de José Ortega y Gasset

The world's most prestigious international designers occupy what is known as *la milla del oro* (the golden mile) along Calle de José Ortega y Gasset, close to the corner with Calle de Serrano. On the south side of the street, there's Giorgio Armani and Chanel. Just across the road is Louis Vuitton and Cartier. And that's just the start...

❽ El Lateral

This chic **wine bar** (☑91 435 06 04; www.lateral.com; Calle de Velázquez 57; tapas €1.55-7.65; ☉noon-1am Sun-Wed, noon-2am Thu-Sat; Ⓜ Velázquez, Núñez de Balboa) is cool in the right places, filled as it is with slick suits and classic wines alongside the new wave of style shaking up the *barrio*. It's a classic perch along one of Salamanca's main boulevards to wind down after a hard day's shopping.

400 m
0.2 miles

Av de América

C de Cea Bermúdez
C de Ardemans
C de Béjar

C de Francisco Silvela

Av de
América

C de Diego de León

Diego
de León

C de Padilla

C de José Ortega y

C de Maldonado

C de Juan Bravo

C del General Díaz Portier

C del Príncipe de Vergara

12

Núñez de
Balboa

CASTELLANA

C de María de Molina

C de General Oráa

C de Castelló

C de Claudio Coello

C de Núñez de Balboa

C de Velázquez

**Museo Lázaro
Galdiano**

C de Lagasca

SALAMANCA

4
Fundación
Juan March

C de López de Hoyos

Núñez de
Balboa

C de Padilla

21

C del Pinar

9

C de Serrano

3 Museo al
Aire Libre

C de José Ortega y Gasset

C de Álvarez
de Baena

Glorieta
de Emilio
Castelar

CHAMBERÍ

C de Rafael Calvo

Plaza del
Doctor
Marañón

Gregorio
Marañón

Glorieta de
Rubén Darío

Rubén
Darío

C de Jenner

ALMAGRO

91

For reviews see

🔴	Top Sights	p86
🔵	Sights	p92
✖	Eating	p94
🔴	Drinking	p95
🔴	Shopping	p96

C de Alcátara

GOYA

Plaza de
Salvador
Dalí

Ⓜ Goya

C del Conde de Peñalver

C de Don Ramón de la Cruz

C de Ayala

C de la Hermosilla

C de Goya

11

C de Alcalá

Ⓜ Goya

C de Narváez

C del Duque de Sesto

C de O'Donnell

C del General Pardiñas

C del Príncipe de Vergara

C de Jorge Juan

Príncipe
de Vergara

Av de Menéndez Pelayo

C del General Díaz Porlier

Ibiza Ⓜ

C de Castelló

C de Núñez de Balboa

Paseo del Duque
de Fernán Núñez

16 ⓞ ✖ 8

Ⓜ Velázquez

C de Velázquez

15 ⓞ

6 ✖ ⓞ

Paseo de la Castellana

C de Zurbara

C de Fernando
el Santo

C de Ayala

RECOLETOS

C de la Hermosilla

C de Goya

C de Claudio Coello

C de Serrano

C de Jorge Juan

13 ⓞ
14 ⓞ

19 ⓞ

17 ⓞ

20 ⓞ
18 ⓞ

Museo 7 ✖

2 Arqueológico
Nacional

C de Villanueva

JUSTICIA

C del Conde de Aranda

C de Columela

C de Alcalá

10 Ⓜ

Ⓜ Colón

Ⓜ Serrano

Jardines de
Descubrimiento

Biblioteca
Nacional &
Museo del Libro

1 ⓞ

C del Cid

C de Villanueva

Chi
Spa

5 ⓞ

Retiro Ⓜ

Parque
del Buen
Retiro

Paseo de los Recoletos

C de los Recoletos

C de Salustiano

Plaza de la
Independencia

E

D

C

B

A

5

6

7

8

Sights

Biblioteca Nacional
& Museo del Libro LIBRARY, MUSEUM

1 ⊙ Map p90, A7

Perhaps the most impressive of the grand edifices erected along the Paseo de los Recoletos in the 19th century, the 1892 Biblioteca Nacional (National Library) dominates the southern end of Plaza de Colón. Downstairs, and entered via a separate entrance, the fascinating and recently overhauled museum is a must for bibliophiles, with interactive displays on printing presses and other materials, illuminated manuscripts, the history of the library, and literary cafes. (☏91 580 78 05; www.bne.es; Paseo de los Recoletos 20; admission free; ⊙library 9am-9pm Mon-Fri, 9am-2pm Sat mid-Sep–mid-Jun, 9am-7.30pm Mon-Fri mid-Jun–mid-Sep, museum 10am-8pm Tue-Sat, 10am-2pm Sun; ⓂColón)

Ⓠ Local Life
Mercado de la Paz

One of few Madrid markets to have been gentrified in recent years, **Mercado de la Paz** (off Calle de Ayala; ⊙9am-8pm Mon-Sat) remains a thoroughly local market. Fresh produce, meat and fish are the mainstays, but there's plenty of things to buy and eat as you go (cured meats and cheeses, for example).

Museo Arqueológico
Nacional MUSEUM

2 ⊙ Map p90, A7

Reopened after a massive overhaul of the building, the showpiece National Archaeology Museum contains a sweeping accumulation of artefacts behind its towering facade. Daringly redesigned within, the museum ranges across Spain's ancient history and the large collection includes stunning mosaics taken from Roman villas across Spain, intricate Muslim-era and Mudéjar handiwork, sculpted figures such as the *Dama de Ibiza* and *Dama de Elche,* examples of Romanesque and Gothic architectural styles and a partial copy of the prehistoric cave paintings of Altamira (Cantabria). (man.mcu.es; Calle de Serrano 13; admission €3, 2-8pm Sat, 9.30am-noon Sun free; ⊙9.30am-8pm Tue-Sat, 9.30am-3pm Sun; ⓂSerrano)

Museo al Aire Libre SCULPTURE

3 ⊙ Map p90, B3

This fascinating open-air collection of 17 abstract sculptures includes works by the renowned Basque artist Eduardo Chillida, the Catalan master Joan Miró, as well as Eusebio Sempere and Alberto Sánchez, one of Spain's foremost sculptors of the 20th century. The sculptures are beneath the overpass where Paseo de Eduardo Dato crosses Paseo de la Castellana, but somehow the hint of traffic grime and pigeon shit only adds to the ap-

Biblioteca Nacional and Museo del Libro

peal. All but one are on the eastern side of Paseo de la Castellana. (Paseo de la Castellana; admission free; ⊙24hr; Ⓜ Rubén Darío)

Fundación Juan March   MUSEUM, CULTURAL CENTRE

4 ◉ Map p90, C4

This foundation organises some of the better temporary exhibitions in Madrid each year and it's always worth checking its website to see what's on or around the corner. It also stages **concerts** (www.march.es; Calle de Castelló 77; admission free; Ⓜ Núñez de Balboa) across a range of musical genres and other events throughout the year.

(www.march.es; Calle de Castelló 77; admission free; ⊙11am-8pm Mon-Sat, 10am-2pm Sun & holidays; Ⓜ Núñez de Balboa)

Chi Spa   SPA

5 ◉ Map p90, B7

Wrap up in a robe and slippers and prepare to be pampered in one of Spain's best day spas. There are separate areas for men and women, and services include a wide range of massages, facials, manicures and pedicures. Now, what was it you were stressed about? (✆91 578 13 40; www.thechispa.com; Calle del Conde de Aranda 6; ⊙10am-8pm Mon-Sat; Ⓜ Retiro)

Eating

La Colonial de Goya
TAPAS €€

6 Map p90, C7

Other better-known places have come and gone around here, but La Colonial de Goya has stood the test of time. The food ranges across the creative (prawn and beef meatballs or broadbean and octopus risotto, for example) to the more traditional (such as warm canapés and *croquetas*). (☏91 575 63 06; www.lacolonialdegoya.com; Calle de Jorge Juan 34; mains €11-22; ☺1-4pm & 8pm-midnight; ⓂVelázquez)

Biotza
TAPAS, BASQUE €€

7 Map p90, B7

This breezy Basque tapas bar is one of the best places in Madrid to sample the creativity of bite-sized *pintxos* (Basque tapas) as only the Basques can make them. It's the perfect combination of San Sebastián–style tapas, Madrid-style pale-green/red-black decoration and unusual angular benches. The

prices quickly add up, but it's highly recommended nonetheless. (☏91 781 03 13; Calle de Claudio Coello 27; cold/hot pintxos €2.80/3.40, raciónes from €6, set menus from €18; ☺1-5pm & 8pm-midnight Mon-Sat; ⓂSerrano)

La Cocina de María Luisa
CASTILIAN €€

8 Map p90, C7

The home kitchen of former parliamentarian María Luisa Banzo has one of Salamanca's most loyal followings. The cooking is a carefully charted culinary journey through Castilla y León, accompanied by well-chosen regional wines and rustic decor that add much warmth to this welcoming place. The house speciality comes from María Luisa's mother – pigs' trotters filled with meat and black truffles from Soria. (☏91 781 01 80; www.lacocinademarialuisa.es; Calle de Jorge Juan 42; mains €17-27; ☺1.30-4pm & 9pm-midnight Mon-Sat Sep-Jul; ⓂVelázquez)

José Luis
SPANISH €€

9 Map p90, B2

With numerous branches around Madrid, José Luis is famous for its fidelity to traditional Spanish recipes. It wins many people's vote for Madrid's best *tortilla de patatas* (Spanish potato omelette), but it's also good for *croquetas* and *ensaladilla rusa* (Russian salad). This outpost along Calle de Serrano has a slightly stuffy, young-men-in-suits feel to it, which is, after all,

---

☑ Top Tip

Pollie-Watch

María Luisa Banzo, the owner of La Cocina de María Luisa, was formerly a prominent figure in the government of conservative Popular Party Prime Minister José María Aznar. Keep an eye out for the former PM (also from Castilla y León) and other prominent politicians in her restaurant.

very Salamanca. (☎91 563 09 58; www.joseluis.es; Calle de Serrano 89; tapas from €5; ⏱8.30am-1am Mon-Fri, 9am-1am Sat, 12.30pm-1am Sun; Ⓜ Gregorio Marañón)

Arriba
MODERN SPANISH €€€

10 ✕ Map p90, A6

Up on the 1st floor of the Platea development, just off Plaza de Colón, this exciting restaurant by the two-Michelin-starred celebrity chef Ramón Freixa has a bistro feel, with a what's-fresh-in-the-market approach to cooking and dishes whose origins range from Catalonia all the way down to Andalucía. (☎91 219 23 05; www.restaurantearriba.com; 1st fl, Calle de Goya 5; mains €17-32; ⏱1.30-4.30pm & 8.30pm-midnight; Ⓜ Serrano, Colón)

Drinking

Geographic Club
BAR

11 🍷 Map p90, D6

With its elaborate stained-glass windows, ethno-chic from all over the world and laid-back atmosphere, the Geographic Club is an excellent choice in Salamanca for an early evening drink – try one of the 30-plus tropical cocktails. We like the table built around an old hot-air-balloon basket almost as much as the cavern-like pub downstairs. (☎91 578 08 62; www.thegeographicclub.es; Calle de Alcalá 141; ⏱1pm-2am Sun-Thu, to 3am Fri & Sat; Ⓜ Goya)

Platea

The ornate cinema named Carlos III opposite the Plaza de Colón has been artfully transformed into, **Platea** (☎91 577 00 25; www.plateamadrid.com; Calle de Goya 5-7; ⏱12.30pm-12.30am Sun-Wed, to 2.30am Thu-Sat; Ⓜ Serrano, Colón), a dynamic culinary scene with more than a hint of burlesque. Working with the original theatre-style layout, the developers have ensured that the all tables in some way face the stage across the soaring open central space where cabaret-style or 1930s-era performances or live cooking shows provide a rather glamorous backdrop. The chefs to have opened up here boast six Michelin stars among them, and there are 12 restaurants, three gourmet food stores and cocktail bars.

Almonte
CLUB

12 🍷 Map p90, D3

If flamenco has captured your soul, but you're keen to do more than watch, head to Almonte. Live acts kick the night off, paying homage to the flamenco roots of Almonte in Andalucía's deep south. The young and the beautiful who come here have *sevillanas* (a flamenco dance style) in their soul and in their feet. (☎91 563 25 04; www.almontesalarociera.com; Calle de Juan Bravo 35; ⏱10pm-5am Sun-Fri, 10pm-6am Sat; Ⓜ Núñez de Balboa, Diego de León)

Serrano 41　　　　　　CLUB

13 🚇 Map p90, B5

If bullfighters, Real Madrid stars and other A-listers can't drag themselves away from Salamanca, chances are that you'll find them here, although the glamour has waned a little of late. Danceable pop and house dominate Friday and Saturday nights, funk gets a turn on Sunday. Admission from €12. (📞687 871045; www.serrano41.com; Calle de Serrano 41; ⏰11pm-5.30am Wed-Sun; Ⓜ Serrano)

Shopping

De Viaje　　　　　　BOOKS

14 🔒 Map p90, B5

Whether you're after a guidebook, a coffee-table tome or travel literature, De Viaje, Madrid's largest travel bookshop, probably has it. Covering every region of the world, it has mostly Spanish titles, but plenty in English as well. (📞91 577 98 99; www.deviaje.com; Calle de Serrano 41; ⏰10am-8.30pm Mon-Fri, 10.30am-2.30pm & 5-8pm Sat; Ⓜ Serrano)

☑️ Top Tip

Plan for a Picnic

Mallorca (📞91 577 18 59; www.pasteleria-mallorca.com; Calle de Serrano 6; mains €7-12; ⏰9am-9pm; Ⓜ Retiro) has fantastic takeaway foods, ideal if you're planning a picnic in the Parque del Buen Retiro, which borders Salamanca to the south.

Ekseption & Eks　　　CLOTHING, ACCESSORIES

15 🔒 Map p90, C6

This elegant showroom store consistently leads the way with the latest trends, spanning catwalk designs alongside a look that is more informal, though always sophisticated. The unifying theme is urban chic and its list of designer brands includes Balenciaga, Givenchy, Marc Jacobs and Dries van Noten. Next door is the preserve of younger, more casual lines, including a fantastic selection of jeans. (📞91 361 97 76; www.ekseption.es; Calle de Velázquez 28; ⏰10.30am-2.30pm & 4.30-8.30pm Mon-Sat; Ⓜ Velázquez)

Gallery　　　　CLOTHING, ACCESSORIES

16 🔒 Map p90, C7

This stunning showpiece of men's and women's fashions and accessories (shoes, bags, belts and the like) is the new Madrid in a nutshell – stylish, brand conscious and all about having the right look. There are creams and fragrances, as well as quirkier items such as designer crash helmets. With an interior designed by Tomas Alia, it's one of the city's coolest shops. (📞91 576 79 31; www.gallerymadrid.com; Calle de Jorge Juan 38; ⏰10.30am-8.30pm Mon-Sat; Ⓜ Príncipe de Vergara, Velázquez)

Isolée　　　　　　FOOD, FASHION

17 🔒 Map p90, B5

Multipurpose lifestyle stores were late in coming to Madrid, but they're now all the rage and there's none more stylish than Isolée. It sells a select range of everything from clothes (Andy Warhol to Adidas) and shoes to CDs and food. (☏902 876 136; www.isolee.com; Calle de Claudio Coello 55; ◷11am-8.30pm Mon-Fri, 11am-9pm Sat; Ⓜ Serrano)

Loewe   FASHION

18 🔒 Map p90, B6

Born in 1846 in Madrid, Loewe is arguably Spain's signature line in high-end fashion. Classy handbags and accessories are the mainstays and prices can be jaw-droppingly high, but it's worth stopping by here, even if you don't plan to buy. (☏91 426 35 88; www.loewe.com; Calle de Serrano 26 & 34; ◷10am-8.30pm Mon-Sat; Ⓜ Serrano)

Mantequería Bravo   FOOD, WINE

19 🔒 Map p90, B5

Behind the attractive old facade lies a connoisseur's paradise, filled with local cheeses, sausages, wines and coffees. The products here are great for a gift, but everything's so good that you won't want to share. Not that

long ago, Mantequería Bravo won the prize for Madrid's best gourmet food shop or delicatessen – it's as simple as that. (www.bravo1931.com; Calle de Ayala 24; ◷9.30am-2.30pm & 5.30-8.30pm Mon-Fri, 9.30am-2.30pm Sat; Ⓜ Serrano)

Purificación García   FASHION

20 🔒 Map p90, B6

Fashions may come and go but Puri consistently manages to keep ahead of the pack. Her signature style for men and women is elegant and mature designs that are just as at home in the workplace as at a wedding. (☏91 435 80 13; www.purificaciongarcia.com; Calle de Serrano 28; ◷10am-8.30pm Mon-Sat; Ⓜ Serrano)

Balenciaga   FASHION

21 🔒 Map p90, B4

Flagship store for the celebrated Basque Balenciaga brand, with a stunning limestone-and-marble interior. (☏91 419 99 00; www.balenciaga.com; Calle de Lagasca 75; ◷10.30am-8pm Mon-Sat; Ⓜ Núñez de Balboa)

Top Sights
Plaza de Toros & Museo Taurino

Getting There

Ⓜ **Metro** Las Ventas Metro station (line 2) sits right outside the bullring – getting there couldn't be easier.

East of central Madrid, the Plaza de Toros Monumental de Las Ventas (often known simply as Las Ventas) is the heart and soul of Spain's bullfighting tradition and, as such, is the most important bullring in the world. To be carried high on the shoulders of aficionados out through the Puerta de Madrid is the ultimate dream of any *torero* (bullfighter) – if you've made it at Las Ventas, you've reached the pinnacle of the bullfighting world.

Don't Miss

Architecture

One of the largest rings in the bullfighting world, Las Ventas has a grand Mudéjar (a Moorish architectural style) exterior and a suitably colosseum-like arena surrounding the broad sandy ring. It was opened in 1931 and hosted its first fight three years later; its four storeys can seat 25,000 spectators.

Puerta de Madrid

The grand and decidedly Moorish Puerta de Madrid symbolises the aspiration of all bullfighters and, suitably, it's known colloquially as the 'Gate of Glory'. Madrid's bullfighting crowd is known as the most demanding in Spain – if they carry a *torero* out through the gate (usually clutching an ear or a tail – trophies only awarded to an elite few), it's because he has performed exceptionally.

Guided Tours

Guided visits (conducted in English and Spanish) take you out onto the sand and into the royal box; they last 40 minutes and start on the hour. For reservations, contact **Las Ventas Tour** (☎687 739032; www.lasventastour.com; adult/child €14/8; ⏱10am-5.30pm, days of bullfight 10am-1.30pm). The tours are a terrific way to get a feel for the whole experience.

Museo Taurino

To gain some insight into the whole subculture that surrounds bullfighting, wander into the Museo Taurino. Here you'll find a curious collection of paraphernalia, costumes (the *traje de luces*, or suit of lights, is one of bullfighting's most recognisable props), photos and other bullfighting memorabilia up on the top floor above one of the two courtyards by the ring.

Calle de Alcalá 237

Ⓜ Ventas

☑ Bullfighting Facts

▶ The bullfighting season runs from around the Fiestas de San Isidro in early May (daily bullfights) through to October (weekends only).

▶ Bullfighting's popularity is waning in Madrid and the average age of paying spectators increases with each passing year.

▶ Even so, bullfights during Madrid's Fiesta de San Isidro remain hugely popular and a Barcelona-style ban is is extremely unlikely.

✕ Take Break

▶ Stop by El Rincón de Jerez for lunch or, better, still for an evening meal and its 11pm spectacular.

▶ There are numerous tapas bars along Calle de Alcalá and surrounding streets – most have walls lined with bullfighting photos.

Explore

Malasaña & Chueca

Malasaña and Chueca are where Madrid gets up close and personal. Yes, there are rewarding museums and examples of landmark architecture sprinkled throughout. But these two inner-city *barrios* are more about doing than seeing. Here, it's more the experience of life as it's lived by *madrileños* than the traditional traveller experience of ticking off a list of attractions.

The Sights in a Day

☀ Start with a coffee at **Gran Café de Gijón** (p110), just as the literati have done for decades. Drop down the hill to Plaza Dos de Mayo, a lovely square that's quiet by day and busy by night – very Malasaña. Stop for a coffee at **Café Manuela** (p110) or **Lolina Vintage Café** (p103) – or both! – then window-shop for retro gear at the **Mercado de Fuencarral** (p102). For lunch, take your pick between **La Mucca de Pez** (p107) or **Albur** (p108).

☀ After lunch wander down into Chueca, pausing to admire the **Sociedad General de Autores y Editores** (p106), before visiting the **Museo de Historia** (p106). Then find out what Chueca's all about at **Diurno** (p111).

☽ Gay Chueca eases into the night at **Café Acuarela** (p110), while a tapas crawl for dinner could take in **Bocaito** (p108), or try **Bazaar** (p106) for a sit-down meal. Storied cocktail bars abound, but none rival world-famous **Museo Chicote** (p108). **La Vía Láctea** (p103) is very Malasaña, whereafter we love **El Junco Jazz Club** (p112) to see us through until dawn.

For a local's day in Malasaña, see p102.

○ Local Life

Counterculture in Malasaña (p102)

♥ Best of Malasaña & Chueca

Retro Fashions
Mercado de Fuencarral (p102)

Snapo (p113)

El Templo de Susu (p113)

Gay Chuenca
Café Acuarela (p110)

Why Not? (p111)

Black & White (p112)

Cocktail Bars
Museo Chicote (p108)

Del Diego (p110)

Getting There

Ⓜ **Metro** For Malasaña, the best stations are Bilbao (lines 1 and 4), Tribunal (lines 1 and 10), San Bernardo (2 and 4) and Noviciado (2). Chueca station (line 5) is in the heart of the *barrio* of the same name, while Alonso Martínez (4, 5 and 10) can be useful. Gran Vía (1 and 5) is good for both Malasaña and Chueca.

Local Life
Counterculture in Malasaña

Malasaña was the epicentre of *la movida madrileña* (the Madrid scene) in the 1980s, and that spirit lives on here. Partly it survives in retro bars, nightclubs and shops that pay homage to the '70s and '80s. But there's also a 'new' and appealing trend towards the vintage aspect of Malasaña life. The common theme is the alternative slant these places take on life in their bid to relive or re-create the past.

① Mercado de Fuencarral
Madrid's home of alternative club cool, **Mercado de Fuencarral** (www. mdf.es; Calle de Fuencarral 45; ⊘11am-9pm Mon-Sat; Ⓜ Tribunal) is still going strong, revelling in its reverse snobbery. With shops like Fuck, Ugly Shop and Black Kiss, it's funky, grungy and filled to the rafters with torn T-shirts, black leather and silver studs. When it was threatened with closure in 2008, there was nearly an uprising.

2 Retro City

Malasaña down to its Dr Martens, **Retro City** (Calle de Corredera Alta de San Pablo 4; ⊗noon-2.30pm & 5.30-9pm Mon-Sat; ⓂTribunal), with its 'vintage for the masses', lives for the colourful '70s and '80s. Whereas other stores in the *barrio* have gone for an angry, thumb-your-nose-at-society look, Retro City just looks back with nostalgia.

3 Lolina Vintage Café

Lolina Vintage Café (☑91 523 58 59; www.lolinacafe.com; Calle del Espíritu Santo 9; ⊗10am-12.30am Sun-Thu, 10am-2am Fri & Sat; ⓂTribunal) captures the essence of the *barrio* in one small space. With a studied retro look (comfy old-style chairs and sofas, gilded mirrors and 1970s-era wallpaper), it confirms that the new Malasaña is not unlike the old.

4 Casa Julio

A city-wide poll for Madrid's best *croquetas* (croquettes; fried rolls with filling) would see half voting for **Casa Julio** (☑91 522 72 74; Calle de la Madera 37; 6/12 croquetas €5/10; ⊗1-3.30pm & 6.30-11pm Mon-Sat Sep-Jul; ⓂTribunal) and the remainder not doing so because they haven't been yet. There's the traditional *jamón* (ham) variety or more creative choices.

5 Bar Palentino

Formica tables, no attention to detail, and yet...**Bar Palentino** (☑91 532 30 58; Calle del Pez 8; bocadillos €1.80-2.50; ⊗7am-2pm Mon-Sat; ⓂNoviciado) is an ageless Malasaña bar wildly popular with young and old alike. Its irresistible charm derives from its tables, and owners María Dolores (she claims to be 'the house speciality') and Casto.

6 Tupperware

A Malasaña stalwart and prime candidate for the bar that best catches the enduring *rockero* spirit of Malasaña, **Tupperware** (☑91 446 42 04; www.tupperwareclub.com; Calle de la Corredera Alta de San Pablo 26; ⊗9pm-3am Mon-Wed, 8pm-3.30am Thu-Sat, 8pm-3am Sun; ⓂTribunal) draws a 30-something crowd, spins indie rock with a bit of soul and classics from the '60s and '70s, and generally revels in its kitsch.

7 La Vía Láctea

A living, breathing and delightfully grungy relic of *la movida*, **La Vía Láctea** (☑91 446 75 81; Calle de Velarde 18; ⊗8pm-3am Sun-Thu, 8pm-3.30am Fri & Sat; ⓂTribunal) remains a Malasaña favourite for an informal crowd that lives for the 1980s. The music ranges across rock, pop, garage, rockabilly and indie. Expect long queues on weekends.

8 Plaza Dos de Mayo

Named after the Malasaña uprising against French occupation in 1808 and still a hub of *barrio* life, Plaza Dos de Mayo has a warm, rebellious spirit. By day it's the preserve of dog-walkers and families, but by night the crowds spill from neighbouring bars onto the plaza to celebrate the freedom of living Madrid. Very Malasaña.

E **F** **G** **H**

C de Santa Engracia

0 — 0
400 m
0.2 miles

C de Nicasio Gallego

C de Manuel Silvela

C de Francisco de Rojas

Bilbao

C de Eguilaz

C de José Marañón

C de Almagro

C de Zurbano

C de Fernando el Santo

C de Sagasta

C de Manuel González Longoria

Plaza de Alonso Martínez

Alonso Martínez

Alonso Martínez

C de Orfila

Paseo de la Castellana

C de Larra

C de Serrano Anguita

C de Mejía Lequerica

C de Apodaca

Plaza de Santa Bárbara

C de Génova

C de Alcalá Galiano

Fuencarral

Museo de Historia **1**

C de la Beneficencia

C de San Mateo

22

C de Hortaleza

20

C de Campoamor

C de Orellana

Plaza de la Villa de París

Plaza de Colón

Tribunal

Jardines Arquitecto Rivera

C de San Lorenzo

2 Sociedad General de Autores y Editores

C de Argensola

C del General Castaños

C del Marqués de la Ensenada

Plaza de San Idefonso

C de la Santa Brígida

C de Pelayo

13

C de Belén

Plaza de las Salesas

C de Bárbara de Braganza

de Colón

C de la Farmacia

C San Lucas

15

Valverde

C de Hernán Cortés

C de Augusto Figueroa

CHUECA

C de Gravina

C de Piamonte

C del Conde de Xiquena

21

C de Fuencarral

C de Hortaleza

10

Chueca

18

C del Almirante

C de Tamayo y Baus

14

C del Cid

17

C de Barbieri

25

C de la Libertad

C de Prim

Paseo de los Recoletos

C de San Marcos

3 **16**

C de Barquillo

C de Salustiano

C de la Libertad

8

Plaza del Rey

Paseo del Prado

Gran Via

C de Clavel

12

C de las Infantas

9

C de la Reina

Gran Via

Banco de España

Plaza de la Red de San Luis

C del Caballero de Gracia

de los Jardines

CENTRO

Sevilla

C de Alcalá

C de la Aduana

Banco de España

For reviews see	
◉ Sights	p106
✕ Eating	p106
○ Drinking	p108
✦ Entertainment	p112
◢ Shopping	p112

Sights

Museo de Historia   MUSEUM

1 ◎ Map p104, E2

The fine Museo de Historia (formerly the Museo Municipal) has an elaborate and restored baroque entrance, raised in 1721 by Pedro de Ribera. Behind this facade, the collection is dominated by paintings and other memorabilia charting the historical evolution of Madrid. The highlights are Goya's *Allegory of the City of Madrid* (on the 1st floor), the caricatures lampooning Napoleon and the early 19th-century French occupation of Madrid (1st floor), and the expansive model of Madrid as it was in 1830 (basement). (📞91 701 16 86; www.madrid.es/museodehistoria; Calle de Fuencarral 78; admission free; ⏱11am-2pm & 4-7pm Tue-Fri, 10am-2pm & 4-7pm Sat & Sun; Ⓜ Tribunal)

☑ Top Tip
Two Dinner Sittings

In order to make the most of their popularity, some restaurants in Malasaña and elsewhere offer two sittings on Friday and Saturday nights, usually around 9pm and 11pm. Unless you can't wait, we recommend reserving a table for the second sitting — otherwise you'll often get the feeling that they're trying to hurry you along.

Sociedad General de Autores y Editores   ARCHITECTURE

2 ◎ Map p104, F3

This swirling, melting wedding cake of a building is as close as Madrid comes to the work of Antoni Gaudí, which so illuminates Barcelona. It's a joyously self-indulgent ode to *modernismo* and is virtually one of a kind in Madrid. Casual visitors are actively discouraged, although what you see from the street is impressive enough. The only exceptions are on the first Monday of October, International Architecture Day, when its interior staircase alone is reason enough to come. (General Society of Authors & Editors; Calle de Fernando VI 4; Ⓜ Alonso Martínez)

Eating

Bazaar   MODERN SPANISH €

3 ✖ Map p104, F4

Bazaar's popularity among the well-heeled Chueca set shows no sign of abating. Its pristine white interior design, with theatre-style lighting and wall-length windows, may draw a crowd that looks like it's stepped out of the pages of *¡Hola!* magazine, but the food is extremely well priced and innovative, and the atmosphere is casual. (📞91 523 39 05; www.restaurantbazaar.com; Calle de la Libertad 21; mains €6.50-10; ⏱1.15-4pm & 8.30-11.30pm Sun-Wed, 1.15-4pm & 8.15pm-midnight Thu-Sat; Ⓜ Chueca)

Museo de Historia

Bodega de la Ardosa

TAPAS €

4  Map p104, E3

Going strong since 1892, the charming, wood-panelled bar of Bodega de la Ardosa is brimful of charm. To come here and not try the *salmorejo* (cold tomato soup made with bread, oil, garlic and vinegar), *croquetas* (croquettes) or *tortilla de patatas* (potato and onion omelette) would be a crime. On weekend nights there's scarcely room to move. (☑91 521 49 79; www.laardosa.es; Calle de Colón 13; tapas & raciónes €4-11; ⊗8.30am-2am Mon-Fri, 12.45pm-2.30am Sat & Sun; Ⓜ Tribunal)

La Mucca de Pez

SPANISH, TAPAS €€

5  Map p104, D3

The only problem with this place is that it's such an agreeable spot to spend an afternoon, it can be impossible to snaffle a table. An ample wine list complements the great salads, creative pizzas and a good mix of meat and seafood mains, while the atmosphere makes it all taste even better. (☑91 521 00 00; www.lamucca.es; Plaza Carlos Cambronero 4; mains €9-16; ⊗1pm-1am Mon-Fri, 1pm-2am Sat & Sun; Ⓜ Callao)

La Gastrocroquetería de Chema

TAPAS €€

6 ✗ Map p104, D4

Croquetas in all their glory are what this place is all about. Try the classic version (made with *jamón* or cod) or any number of riffs on the croquette theme (with *sobrasada* – spreadable cured meat – and chocolate, for example). It also does other tapas, with a couple of set menus to guide your way. (📞91 364 22 63; www.gastrocroqueteria. com; Calle del Barco 7; tapas €3-13, set menus €16-28; ⏱9pm-midnight Mon-Fri, 2-4.30pm & 9pm-midnight Sat & Sun; Ⓜ Tribunal)

Albur

TAPAS, SPANISH €€

7 ✗ Map p104, D1

One of Malasaña's best deals, this place has a wildly popular tapas bar and a classy but casual restaurant out the back. The restaurant waiters never seem to lose their cool, and their ex-

Ⓠ Local Life
Bon Vivant

Every now and then we stumble upon a local haunt that captures the essence of an entire *barrio*. **Bon Vivant & Co** (Map p105, F3; 📞91 704 82 86; www.bonvivantco.es; Calle de San Gregorio 8; mains €9-15; ⏱9am-1am Mon-Fri, 10am-2am Sat & Sun; Ⓜ Chueca) is such a place. Set on a tiny square, it serves up casual light meals in a classy but quietly intimate atmosphere that is typical of daytime Chueca.

tremely well-priced rice dishes are the stars of the show, although in truth you could order anything here and leave well satisfied. (📞91 594 27 33; www.res-taurantealbur.com; Calle de Manuela Malasaña 15; mains €11-16; ⏱1-5pm & 8pm-12.30am Mon-Fri, 1pm-1am Sat & Sun; Ⓜ Bilbao)

Bocaito

TAPAS €€

8 ✗ Map p104, F4

Film-maker Pedro Almodóvar once described this traditional bar and restaurant as 'the best antidepressant'. Forget about the sit-down restaurant (which is nonetheless well regarded) and jam into the bar, shoulder-to-shoulder with the casual crowd, order a few Andalucian *raciones* off the menu and slosh them down with some gritty red or a *caña* (small glass of beer). (📞91 532 12 19; www.bocaito.com; Calle de la Libertad 4-6; tapas €2-8, mains €10-29; ⏱1-4pm & 8.30pm-midnight Mon-Sat; Ⓜ Chueca, Sevilla)

Drinking

Museo Chicote

COCKTAIL BAR

9 Ⓤ Map p104, E5

This place is a Madrid landmark, complete with its 1930s-era interior, and its founder is said to have invented more than 100 cocktails, which the likes of Hemingway, Ava Gardner, Grace Kelly, Sophia Loren and Frank Sinatra have all enjoyed at one time or another. (📞91 532 67 37; grupomercadodelareina.com/en/museo-chicote-en/; Gran Vía 12; ⏱5pm-3am Mon-Thu, to 3.30am Fri & Sat; Ⓜ Gran Vía)

Understand

La Movida Madrileña

What London was to the swinging '60s and Paris to 1968, Madrid was to the 1980s. After the long, dark years of dictatorship and conservative Catholicism, the death of Franco and the advent of democracy, Spaniards, especially *madrileños*, were prompted to emerge onto the streets with all the zeal of ex-convent schoolgirls. Nothing was taboo in a phenomenon known as *la movida madrileña* (literally 'the Madrid scene') as young *madrileños* discovered the '60s, '70s and '80s all at once. Drinking, drugs and sex suddenly were OK. All-night partying was the norm, drug taking in public was not a criminal offence (that changed in 1992) and the city howled.

What was remarkable about *la movida* was that it was presided over by Enrique Tierno Galván, an ageing former university professor who had been a leading opposition figure under Franco and was affectionately known throughout Spain as 'the old teacher'. A Socialist, he became mayor in 1979 and, for many, launched *la movida* by telling a public gathering *'a colocarse y ponerse al loro'*, which loosely translates as 'get stoned and do what's cool'. Unsurprisingly, he was Madrid's most popular mayor ever, and when he died in 1986, a million *madrileños* turned out for his funeral.

La movida was not just about rediscovering the Spanish art of *salir de copas* (going out for a drink). It was also accompanied by an explosion of creativity among the country's musicians, designers and film-makers, who were keen to shake off the shackles of the repressive Franco years. By one tally, Madrid was home to 300 rock bands and 1500 fashion designers during *la movida*. The most famous of these was film director Pedro Almodóvar. Although his later films became internationally renowned, his first films, *Pepi, Luci, Bom y otras chicas del montón* (Pepi, Luci, Bom and the Other Girls; 1980) and *Laberinto de pasiones* (Labyrinth of Passions; 1982), are where the spirit of the movement really comes alive.

At the height of *la movida* in 1981, Andy Warhol openly regretted that he could not spend the rest of his days here. In 1985, the *New York Times* anointed the Spanish capital 'the new cultural capital of the world and the place to be'. Things have quietened down a little since those heady days, but you'll only notice if you were here during the 1980s...

Café Acuarela

CAFE

10 | Map p104, F3

A few steps up the hill from Plaza de Chueca and long a centrepiece of gay Madrid – a huge statue of a nude male angel guards the doorway – this is an agreeable, dimly lit salon decorated with, among other things, religious icons. (📞91 522 21 43; www.cafeacuarela. es; Calle de Gravina 10; ⏰11am-2am Sun-Thu, 11am-3am Fri & Sat; Ⓜ Chueca)

Café Manuela

CAFE

11 | Map p104, D2

Stumbling into this graciously restored throwback to the 1950s along one of Malasaña's grittier streets is akin to discovering hidden treasure. There's a luminous quality to it when you come in out of the night and, like so many Madrid cafes, it's a surprisingly multifaceted space, serving cocktails, delicious milkshakes and offering board games atop the marble tables. (📞91 531 70 37; Calle de San Vicente Ferrer 29; ⏰4pm-2am Sun-Thu, 4pm-2.30am Fri & Sat; Ⓜ Tribunal)

Del Diego

COCKTAIL BAR

12 | Map p104, E5

Del Diego is one of the city's most celebrated cocktail bars. The decor blends old-world cafe with New York style, and it's the sort of place where the music rarely drowns out the conversation. Even with around 75 cocktails to choose from, we'd still order the signature 'El Diego' (vodka, advocaat, apricot brandy and lime). (📞91 523 31 06; www.deldiego.com; Calle de la Reina 12; ⏰7pm-3am Mon-Thu, 7pm-3.30am Fri & Sat; Ⓜ Gran Vía)

Café Belén

BAR

13 | Map p104, F3

Café Belén is cool in all the right places – lounge and chill-out music, dim lighting, a great range of drinks (the mojitos are especially good) and a low-key crowd that's the height of casual sophistication. It's one of our preferred Chueca watering holes. (📞91 308 27 47; elcafebelen.com; Calle de Belén 5; ⏰3.30pm-3am Tue-Thu, 3.30pm-3.30am Fri, 1pm-3.30am Sat, 1-10pm Sun; Ⓜ Chueca)

Gran Café de Gijón

CAFE

14 | Map p104, H4

This graceful old cafe has been serving coffee and meals since 1888 and has long been favoured by Madrid's literati for a drink or a meal – *all* of Spain's great 20th-century literary figures came here for coffee and *tertulias* (social gatherings). You'll find yourself among intellectuals, conservative Franco diehards and young *madrileños* looking for a quiet drink. (📞91 521 54 25; www.cafegijon.com; Paseo de los Recoletos 21; ⏰7am-1.30am; Ⓜ Chueca, Banco de España)

Café-Restaurante El Espejo

CAFE

15 | Map p104, H3

Once a haunt of writers and intellectuals, this architectural gem blends

Museo Chicote (p108)

Modernista and art deco styles and its interior could well overwhelm you with all the mirrors, chandeliers and bow-tied service of another era. The atmosphere is suitably quiet and refined, although our favourite corner is the elegant glass pavilion out on the Paseo de los Recoletos. (✆91 308 23 47; www.restauranteelespejo.com; Paseo de los Recoletos 31; ⏰8am-midnight; Ⓜ Colón)

Diurno
CAFE

16 Ⓟ Map p104, F4

One of the most important hubs of *barrio* life in Chueca, this cafe (with DVD store attached) has become to modern Chueca what the grand literary cafes were to another age. It's always full

with a fun Chueca crowd relaxing amid the greenery. It also serves well-priced meals and snacks if you can't bear to give up your seat. (✆91 522 00 09; grupomercadodelareina.com/en/diurno-en/; Calle de San Marcos 37; ⏰10am-1am Sun-Thu, 10am-2am Fri & Sat; Ⓜ Chueca)

Why Not?
CLUB

17 Ⓟ Map p104, F4

Underground, narrow and packed with bodies, gay-friendly Why Not? is the sort of place where nothing's left to the imagination (the gay and straight crowd who come here are pretty amorous) and it's full nearly every night of the week. Pop and top-40 music are the standard here, and the dancing crowd is mixed and serious about having a good time. (📞91 521 80 34; www.whynotmadrid.com; Calle de San Bartolomé 7; ⏱10.30pm-6am; Ⓜ️Chueca)

Black & White   GAY, CLUB

18 🚇 Map p104, F4

People *still* talk about the opening party of Black & White way back in 1982, and ever since it's been a pioneer of Chueca's gay nights. This place is extravagantly gay with drag acts, male strippers and a refreshingly no-holds-barred approach to life. (📞91 521 24 92; Calle de la Libertad 34; ⏱10pm-6.30am; Ⓜ️Chueca)

Ya'sta   CLUB

19 🚇 Map p104, E4

Going strong since 1985 and the height of *la movida madrileña*,

Ya'sta is a stalwart of the Malasaña night. Everything gets a run here, from techno, psychedelic trance and electronica to indie pop. Check the website for upcoming sessions. (📞91 521 88 33; www.yastaclub.net; Calle de Valverde 10; admission €10; ⏱11.45pm-6am Wed-Sat; Ⓜ️Gran Vía)

Entertainment

El Junco Jazz Club   JAZZ

20 ⭐ Map p104, F2

El Junco has established itself on the Madrid nightlife scene by appealing as much to jazz aficionados as to clubbers. Its secret is high-quality live jazz gigs from Spain and around the world, followed by DJs spinning funk, soul, nu jazz, blues and innovative groove beats. There are also jam sessions at 11pm in jazz (Tuesday) and blues (Sunday). (📞91 319 20 81; www.eljunco.com; Plaza de Santa Bárbara 10; ⏱10.30pm-5.30am Tue-Thu & Sun, 9pm-6am Fri & Sat, concerts 11pm Tue-Sun; Ⓜ️Alonso Martínez)

Shopping

Custo Barcelona   FASHION

21 🛍 Map p104, E4

The chic shop of Barcelona designer Custo Dalmau wears its Calle de Fuencarral address well, because the now-iconic T-shirts are at once edgy, awash in attitude and artfully displayed. It's not to everyone's taste, but always

---

🔵 Local Life

Calle de Pez

It's been years in the making, but Calle de Pez, down the lower, southern end of Malasaña has become one of the coolest local haunts in Madrid, a beguiling mix of grungy and cool. **1862 Dry Bar** (Map p104, C3; 📞609 531151; Calle del Pez 27; ⏱3.30pm-2am Mon-Thu, 3.30pm-2.30am Fri & Sat, 3.30-10.30pm Sun; Ⓜ️Noviciado), a casual yet achingly trendy cocktail bar, is typical. Around the corner, Calle de Corredera Baja de San Pablo, where it approaches Gran Vía, is undergoing a similar transformation.

worth a look. (☎91 360 46 36; www.custo. com; Calle de Fuencarral 29; ⏲10am-9pm Mon-Sat, noon-8pm Sun; Ⓜ Gran Vía)

Patrimonio Comunal Olivarero

FOOD

22 🔒 Map p104, F2

For picking up some of the country's olive-oil varieties (Spain is the world's largest producer), Patrimonio Comunal Olivarero is perfect. With examples of the extra-virgin variety (and nothing else) from all over Spain, you could spend ages agonising over the choices. The staff know their oil and are happy to help out if you speak a little Spanish. (☎91 308 05 05; www.pco. es; Calle de Mejía Lequerica 1; ⏲10am-2pm & 5-8pm Mon-Fri, 10am-2pm Sat Sep-Jun, 9am-3pm Mon-Sat Jul; Ⓜ Alonso Martínez)

Snapo

CLOTHING, ACCESSORIES

23 🔒 Map p104, D3

Snapo is rebellious Malasaña to its core, thumbing its nose at the niceties of fashion respectability – hardly surprising given that one of its lines of clothing is called Fucking Bastardz Inc. It does jeans, caps and jackets, but its T-shirts are the Snapo trademark; there are even kids' T-shirts for *really* cool parents. (☎91 017 16 72; www.snaposhoponline.com; Calle del Espíritu Santo 6; ⏲11am-2pm & 5-8.30pm Mon-Sat; Ⓜ Tribunal)

✅ Top Tip

Opening Hours

Although they don't advertise it in their opening hours, many shops along Calle de Fuencarral also open on Sundays. Your best chance is usually the first Sunday of the month.

El Templo de Susu

CLOTHING, ACCESSORIES

24 🔒 Map p104, D3

They won't appeal to everyone, but El Templo de Susu's second-hand clothes from the 1960s and 1970s have clearly found a market among Malasaña's too-cool-for-the-latest-fashions types. It's kind of like charity shop meets vintage, which is either truly awful or retro cool, depending on your perspective. (☎91 523 31 22; Calle del Espíritu Santo 1; ⏲10am-2.30pm & 5.30-9pm Mon-Sat; Ⓜ Tribunal)

Casa Postal

ANTIQUES

25 🔒 Map p104, F4

Old postcards, posters, books and other period knick-knacks fill this treasure cave to the rafters. It's a wonderful slice of old Madrid in which to lose yourself. (☎91 532 70 37; www.casapostal.net; Calle de la Libertad 37; ⏲10am-2pm & 5-7.45pm Mon-Fri, 11am-2pm Sat; Ⓜ Chueca)

Top Sights
Ermita de San Antonio de la Florida

Getting There

Ⓜ **Metro** Go to Prínc-
ipe Pío station (lines
6 and 10). The Ermita
de San Antonio de la
Florida is the southern
of two chapels, a
500m walk northwest
along the Paseo de la
Florida.

From the outside, this humble hermitage gives no
hint of the splendour that lies within. But make no
mistake, this small church ranks alongside Madrid's
finest art galleries on the list of must-sees for art
lovers. Recently restored and also known as the
Panteón de Goya, this chapel has frescoed ceilings
painted by Goya in 1798 on the request of Carlos IV.
As such, it's one of the few places where you can see
Goya masterworks in their original setting.

Don't Miss

The Miracle of St Anthony

Figures on the dome depict the miracle of St Anthony. The saint heard word from his native Lisbon that his father had been unjustly accused of murder. The saint was whisked miraculously to his hometown from northern Italy and Goya's painting depicts the moment in which St Anthony calls on the corpse to rise up and absolve his father.

An 18th-Century Madrid Crowd

As interesting as the miracle that forms the frescoes' centrepiece, a typical Madrid crowd swarms around the saint. It was customary in such works that angels and cherubs appear in the cupola, above all the terrestrial activity, but Goya, never one to let himself be confined by the mores of the day, places the human above the divine.

Goya's Tomb

The painter is buried in front of the altar. His remains were transferred in 1919 from Bordeaux (France), where he had died in self-imposed exile in 1828. Oddly, the skeleton exhumed in Bordeaux was missing one important item – the head.

Nearby: Templo de Debod

Up the hill from the Ermita, this Egyptian **temple** (www.madrid.es; Paseo del Pintor Rosales; admission free; ⏱10am-2pm & 6-8pm Tue-Fri, 9.30am-8pm Sat & Sun Apr-Sep, 9.45am-1.45pm & 4.15-6.15pm Tue-Fri, 9.30am-8pm Sat & Sun Oct-Mar; Ⓜ Ventura Rodríguez) was saved from the rising waters of Lake Nasser (Egypt) during the building of the Aswan Dam. After 1968 it was sent block by block to Spain as a gesture of thanks to Spanish archaeologists in the Unesco team that worked to save the monuments.

---

www.sanantoniode laflorida.es

Glorieta de San Antonio de la Florida 5

admission free

⏱10am-8pm Tue-Sun, hours vary Jul & Aug

Ⓜ Príncipe Pío

☑ Top Tips

▶ Check the opening hours as these do vary from the official hours, particularly in July and August.

▶ On 13 June it's a Madrid tradition for seamstresses to come here to pray for a partner, although the tradition now extends to young women from all walks of life.

✕ Take a Break

Casa Mingo (☎91 547 79 18; www.casamingo.es; Paseo de la Florida 34; raciónes €3-11; ⏱11am-midnight; Ⓜ Príncipe Pío), next to the Ermita, is a well-known Asturian cider house. It focuses primarily on its signature dish of *pollo asado* (roast chicken) accompanied by a bottle of cider.

Local Life
Barrio Life in Chamberí

Getting There

M Metro Quevedo (line 2), Bilbao (lines 1 and 4) and Iglesia (line 1) stations all set you up nicely for a visit to the area.

The generally upmarket *barrio* of Chamberí is widely known as one of the most *castizo* (a difficult term to translate, its meaning lies somewhere between traditional and authentic) neighbourhoods of the capital. With its signature plaza, old-style shops and unmistakeable *barrio* feel, it's off the tourist trail and among the best places in Madrid to attempt to understand what makes the city tick.

❶ Plaza de Olavide

Plaza de Olavide (ⓂBilbao, Iglesia, Quevedo) is the hub of Chamberí life with its park benches, playgrounds and outdoor tables. Inside Bar Mentrida at No 3 you'll find a stirring photographic record of the plaza's history.

❷ Old-Fashioned Shopping

A charming old-world shoe store, **Calzados Cantero** (☎91 447 07 35; Plaza de Olavide 12; ⏰9.45am-2pm & 4.45-8.30pm Mon-Fri, 9.45am-2pm Sat) is famous for its rope-soled *alpargatas* (espadrilles), which start from €6. This place is a *barrio* classic, the sort of place that parents bring their children as their own parents did a generation before.

❸ The King's Watchmaker

Relojería Santolaya (☎91 447 25 64; www.relojeriasantolaya.com; Calle Murillo 8; ⏰10am-1pm & 5-8pm Mon-Fri), an old clock repairer founded in 1867, is the official watch repairer to Spain's royalty and heritage properties. There's not much that's for sale, but stop by the tiny shopfront/workshop to admire the dying art of timepiece repairs.

❹ A Surprise Museum

One of Madrid's best-kept secrets, **Museo Sorolla** (☎91 310 15 84; museosorolla.mcu.es; Paseo del General Martínez Campos 37; adult/child €3/free, free Sun & 2-8pm Sat; ⏰9.30am-8pm Tue-Sat, 10am-3pm Sun) is dedicated to the Valencian artist Joaquín Sorolla, who immortalised the clear Mediterranean light of the Valencian coast.

❺ A Barrio Bar

Bodega de la Ardosa (Calle de Santa Engracia 70; raciones from €7; ⏰9am-3pm & 6-11.30pm Thu-Tue) is a fine old relic with an extravagantly tiled facade (complete with shrapnel holes from the Civil War). Come for some of the best traditional Spanish patatas bravas in town.

❻ Chamberí's Missing Station

For years, *madrileños* wondered what happened to their metro station. Abandoned in 1966, **Estación de Chamberí** (⏰11am-1pm & 5-7pm Fri, 10am-2pm Sat & Sun) has finally reopened as a museum piece that re-creates the era of the station's inauguration in 1919.

❼ Old-Style Stationery

Opened in 1905, **Papelería Salazar** (www.papeleriasalazar.es; Calle de Luchana 7-9; ⏰9.30am-1.30pm & 4.30-8pm Mon-Fri, 9.30am-1.30pm Sat) is Madrid's oldest stationery store and a treasure trove filled with old-style Spanish bookplates, First Communion invitations and the like.

❽ Calle de Fuencarral

Calle de Fuencarral between the Glorietas de Bilbao and Quevedo is one of Madrid's iconic thoroughfares. On Sunday mornings, the street is closed to traffic from 8am to 2pm.

❾ Basque Tapas

At journey's end, **Sagaretxe** (www.sagaretxe.com; Calle de Eloy Gonzalo 26; tapas from €2; ⏰noon-5pm & 7pm-midnight; ⓂIglesia) is one of the best Basque *pintxos* (tapas) bars in Madrid. Simply point and your selection will be plated up for you.

Top Sights
San Lorenzo de El Escorial

Getting There

🚆 **Train** A few dozen Renfe C8 trains make the one-hour trip daily from Madrid's Atocha or Chamartín stations to El Escorial.

🚌 **Bus** Take bus 661 or 664 from Madrid's Moncloa Intercambiador de Autobuses.

Home to the majestic monastery and palace complex of San Lorenzo de El Escorial, this one-time royal getaway rises up from the foothills of the mountains that shelter Madrid from the north and west. The prim little town is overflowing with quaint shops, restaurants and hotels, and the fresh, cool air, among other things, has been drawing city dwellers here since the complex was first built on the orders of King Felipe II in the 16th century.

Don't Miss

Historical Background

An understanding of El Escorial's historical story goes a long way. For example, as was the royal prerogative in those days, several villages were torn down to make way for the undertaking, which included a royal palace and a mausoleum for Felipe's parents, Carlos I and Isabel. Architect Juan de Herrera oversaw the project.

First Steps

Resist the urge to rush to the heart of the complex, and linger over the monastery's main entrance on the west side of the complex. Above the gateway a statue of St Lawrence stands watch, holding a symbolic gridiron, the instrument of his martyrdom (he was roasted alive on one).

Patio de los Reyes

After passing St Lawrence and grimacing at his fate, you'll first enter the Patio de los Reyes (Patio of the Kings), which houses the statues of the six kings of Judah. Admiring these statues, it's difficult not to marvel at the arrogance of the Spanish royals who saw nothing amiss in comparing themselves to the great kings of the past.

Basílica

Directly ahead of the Patio de los Reyes lies the sombre basilica. As you enter, look up at the unusual flat vaulting by the choir stalls. Once inside the church proper, turn left to view Benvenuto Cellini's white Carrara marble statue of Christ crucified (1576) – it's one of the most underrated masterpieces of the complex.

El Greco

The remainder of the ground floor contains various treasures, including some tapestries and an

---

☎ 91 890 78 18

www.patrimonionacional.es

adult/concession €10/5, guide/audioguide €4/4, EU citizens free last three hours Wed & Thu

🕓 10am-8pm Apr-Sep, 10am-6pm Oct-Mar, closed Mon

☑ Top Tips

▸ Avoid coming on a weekend, as the town and whole complex can be overwhelmed by daytrippers from Madrid.

▸ Visit the website www.patrimonionacional.es for a wealth of historical detail on the complex.

▸ The local tourist office website (www.sanlorenzoturismo.org) is good for surrounding attractions if you plan to make a day of it.

✕ Take a Break

La Cueva (www.mesonlacueva.com), a block back from the monastery complex, has been around since 1768 and remains a bastion of traditional Castilian cooking (especially roasted meats).

El Greco painting – impressive as it is, it's a far cry from El Greco's dream of decorating the whole complex. He actually came to Spain from Greece in 1577 hoping to get a job decorating El Escorial, although Felipe II rejected him as a court artist.

Two Museums

After wondering at what might have been had El Greco been given a free hand, head downstairs to the northeastern corner of the complex. You pass through the Museo de Arquitectura and the Museo de Pintura. The former tells (in Spanish) the story of how the complex was built, the latter contains 16th- and 17th-century Italian, Spanish and Flemish art.

Up & Down

The route through the monastery takes you upstairs into a gallery known as the Palacio de Felipe II or Palacio de los Austrias. You'll then descend to the 17th-century Panteón de los Reyes (Crypt of the Kings), where almost all Spain's monarchs since Carlos I are interred. Backtracking a little, you're in the Panteón de los Infantes (Crypt of the Princesses).

Salas Capitulares

Stairs lead up from the Patio de los Evangelistas (Patio of the Gospels) to the Salas Capitulares (chapterhouses) in the southeastern corner of the monastery. These bright, airy rooms, whose ceilings are richly frescoed, contain a treasure chest of works

San Lorenzo de El Escorial

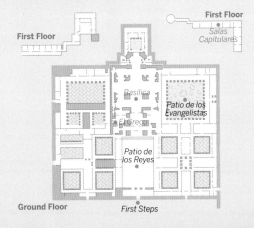

Understand
Developing a Royal Complex

This formidable palace-monastery complex was the brainchild of Spain's King Felipe II (r 1556–1598). Partly conceived as a decadent royal palace and as a mausoleum worthy of Felipe's parents, Carlos I and Isabel, El Escorial was also an announcement to increasingly Protestant Europe that Spain would always be Catholic.

As principal architect, Felipe II chose Juan Bautista de Toledo who had worked on Rome's Basilica of St Peter. The architect's mission was, in the king's words, 'simplicity in the construction, severity in the whole, nobility without arrogance, majesty without ostentation.' In fulfilling these instructions, Juan Bautista de Toledo used locally quarried granite as the primary building material and followed a floor plan based on historical descriptions of Solomon's Temple in Jerusalem.

Several villages were razed to make way for the massive project and the first stone was laid in 1563 (two years after Madrid was chosen as Spain's capital). When Juan Bautista de Toledo died in 1567, architect Juan de Herrera, a towering figure of the Spanish Renaissance, took over the project and saw it through to completion in 1584.

by El Greco, Titian, Tintoretto, José de Ribera and Hieronymus Bosch (known as 'El Bosco' to Spaniards).

Huerta de los Frailes

Just south of the monastery is the **Huerta de los Frailes** (Friars Garden; ⊙10am-7pm Apr-Sep, 10am-6pm Oct-Mar, closed Mon), which merits a stroll. As royal gardens go, it's fairly modest, but can be a wonderfully tranquil spot when the rest of the complex is swarming with visitors.

Jardín del Príncipe

The **Prince's Garden** (admission free; ⊙8am-9.30pm mid-Jun–mid-Aug, shorter hours rest of year), which leads down to the town of El Escorial (and the train station), is a lovely monumental garden and contains the **Casita del Príncipe** (www.patrimonionacional.es; ⊙10am-8pm Apr-Sep, 10am-6pm Oct-Mar, closed Mon), a royal pavilion and small neoclassical gem built in 1772 by Juan de Villanueva under Carlos III for his heir, Carlos IV.

The Best of
Madrid

Palacio de Cristal, Parque del Buen Retiro (p80)
FREDERIC PROCHASSON/GETTY IMAGES ©

Best Walks
Architectural Madrid

🏃 The Walk

Madrid may not have the Eiffel Tower, Colosseum or Sagrada Família, but it is easily the rival of Paris, Rome or Barcelona for its astonishing grand monuments. From the heart of old Madrid where the city was born to the showpiece architecture of 19th- and 20th-century Spain, this walk takes you through the Spanish capital's splendid architectural attractions. Old Madrid boasts its very own style, while the sometimes bombastic, more often graceful, architectural monuments to the past century cut a swath through the centre of the city and down to the Paseo del Prado, one of Europe's most beautiful boulevards.

Start Plaza de la Villa; Ⓜ Ópera

Finish Antigua Estación de Atocha; Ⓜ Atocha Renfe

Length 5km; two to three hours

✖ Take a Break

Estado Puro (Map 82, A3; www.tapasenestadopuro.com; Plaza de Neptuno 4; tapas €5-16, mains €13-22; 🕐 noon–midnight Mon-Sat, noon-4pm Sun; Ⓜ Banco de España)

SYLVAIN SONNET/GETTY IMAGES ©

Museo del Prado (p66)

❶ Plaza de la Villa

This compact **square** (p30) hosts a lovely collection of 17th-century Madrid architecture. The brickwork and slate spires are the most distinctive characteristics of a style known as Madrid baroque (*barroco madrileño*).

❷ Plaza de España

Towering over this square on the east side is the Edificio de España, which clearly sprang from the totalitarian recesses of Franco's imagination such is its resemblance to austere Soviet monumentalism. To the north stands the 35-storey Torre de Madrid, another important landmark on the Madrid skyline.

❸ Gran Vía

The iconic Gran Vía is defined by towering belle époque facades. Eye-catching buildings include the Carrión, Madrid's first tower-block apartment hotel; the 1920s-era Telefónica building used for target practice during the Civil War; and the French-designed 1905 **Edificio Metrópolis** (p56).

❹ Plaza de la Cibeles

Madrid's most striking roundabout is a stirring celebration of the belle époque from the early 20th century. In addition to the extraordinary Palacio de Comunicaciones (1917), the Palacio de Linares, Palacio Buenavista and Banco de España (1891) all watch over the square.

❺ Museo del Prado

The building in which the **Prado** (p66) is housed is itself an architectural masterpiece.

The western wing was designed by Juan de Villanueva, a towering figure of 18th-century Spanish culture and an architect who left his mark across the capital (eg the Plaza Mayor).

❻ Caixa Forum

Caixa Forum (p83), along the Paseo del Prado, is Madrid's most unusual example of contemporary architecture. Its vertical garden, seeming absence of supporting pillars and wrought-iron roof are unlike anything you'll see elsewhere.

❼ Antigua Estación de Atocha

The northwestern wing of Atocha train station was artfully overhauled in 1992. This grand iron-and-glass relic from the 19th century was preserved while its interior was converted into a light-filled tropical garden. It's a thoroughly modern space that nonetheless resonates with the stately European train stations of another age.

Best Walks
Foodie's Madrid

🏃 The Walk

Food is perhaps the most enduring centrepiece of *madrileño* life. In Madrid, arguably the country's most underrated food city, everything great about Spain's culinary traditions and innovations is present, and it's the diverse culinary experiences on offer that make the city such a wonderful introduction to Spanish cuisine. We begin this walk in one of the country's most innovative food markets, wander down to the world's oldest restaurant, walk the length of one of Spain's best tapas streets, shop for wines in one of the city's surviving family bottle shops and then drink sherry in one of Madrid's classic bars.

Start Mercado de San Miguel; **M** Sol

Finish Lhardy; **M** Sol

Length 2km; two to four hours

🍽 Take a Break

Chocolatería de San Ginés (Map 28, D6; ☎ 91 365 65 46; www.chocolateriasangines.com; Pasadizo de San Ginés 5; ⏰ 24hr; **M** Sol)

Mercado de San Miguel (p32)

❶ Mercado de San Miguel

This wonderfully converted early 20th-century **market** (p32) is a gastronome's paradise, with tapas to be enjoyed on the spot (everything from chocolate to caviar), fresh produce at every turn and a buzz that rarely abates until closing time at 2am. La Casa de Bacalao (Stall 17), for example, is a particular favourite.

❷ Casa Revuelta

Casa Revuelta's (p32) decor hasn't changed in decades, nor has the clientele. They come here for the boneless tapas of *bacalao* (cod) and the convivial air of a Madrid bar where the staff shout to make themselves heard. To understand this city, come here at 1pm Sunday.

❸ Restaurante Sobrino de Botín

This is the world's oldest continuously functioning **restaurant** (p32). Roasted meats served in a wonderful setting (ask for a table in the vaulted cellar) could easily explain its longevity, but El Botín also appears in novels by Ernest Hemingway, Frederick Forsyth and a host of local writers.

④ Calle de la Cava Baja

Calle de la Cava Baja's medieval streetscape follows the path of Madrid's long-disappeared medieval wall. It's also one of the great food streets of the world, home to a slew of tapas bars that makes La Latina one of the best places to eat in the country.

⑤ María Cabello

There are wine shops where a catalogue is handed to you, and then there's **María Cabello** (p63). Staff know their wines here, and they are as comfortable speaking to experts as they are to first-timers keen to sample Spanish wines without knowing where to start.

⑥ La Venencia

La Venencia (p59) is the evocation of an old-style Spanish dream. Here staff pour the sherry straight from the barrel, they're not averse to looking grumpy in the honoured tradition of Spanish bartenders and you can almost smell the dust of decades past.

⑦ Lhardy

It would be a shame to wander around Madrid with food on your mind and not wander in to **Lhardy** (p58). The ground-floor deli is all about planning a picnic in the Parque del Buen Retiro tomorrow or buying cured meats, cheeses and other delicacies to take back home. Doing so is *very* Madrid.

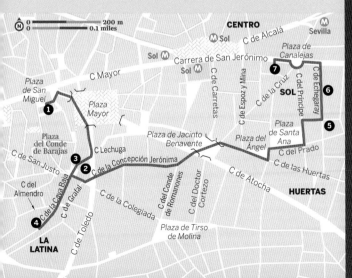

Best
Restaurants

Madrid is arguably the best place to eat in Spain. It's not that the city's culinary traditions are anything special. Rather, everything that is exciting about Spanish cooking finds expression in the capital, from Basque tapas bars to avant garde Catalan chefs, from the best in Galician seafood to Andalucía's Mediterranean catch. Travel from one Spanish village to the next and you'll quickly learn that each has its own speciality. Travel to Madrid and you'll find them all.

MARK READ / LONELY PLANET ©

Madrid Specialities

The city's traditional local cuisine is dominated by hearty stews, particularly in winter, and there are none more hearty than *cocido a la madrileña*, a hotpot or stew that starts with a noodle broth and is followed by, or combined with, carrots, chickpeas, chicken, *morcilla* (blood sausage), beef, lard and possibly other sausage meats, too.

Other popular staples include *cordero asado* (roast lamb), *croquetas* (croquettes), *patatas con huevos fritos* (baked potatoes with eggs, also known as *huevos rotos*), *tortilla de patatas* (a thick potato omelette, pictured above) and endless variations on *bacalao* (cod).

Regional Spanish Cuisine

But this is only half the story. Madrid has wholeheartedly embraced dishes – and the innovations that accompany them – from across the country. Most notably, every day tonnes of fish and seafood are trucked in from Mediterranean and Atlantic ports to satisfy the *madrileño* taste for the sea to the extent that, remarkably for a city so far inland, Madrid is home to the world's second-largest fish market (after Tokyo).

Best for Local Cooking

Taberna La Bola One of the best places in town to try *cocido a la madrileña* and other local favourites such as *callos* (tripe). (p32)

Malacatín A tiled bar where the *cocido* can be tried as a tapas or the more authentic all-you-can-eat version. (p47)

Restaurante Sobrino de Botín The world's oldest restaurant and a hugely atmospheric place to sample roasted meats. (p32)

Lhardy The great and the good of Madrid, from royalty to A-list celebrities, have all eaten in this bastion of traditional cooking. (p58)

Posada de la Villa Another historical converted inn where

Posada de la Villa (p48)

the roasted meats have acquired legendary status across the city. (p48)

Casa Lucio One of Madrid's most celebrated restaurants, where royalty and ordinary *madrileños* order *cocido* and the city's best *huevos rotos*. (p47)

Best for Regional Spanish

Maceiras Earthy decor and good down-home cooking from the coasts of Galicia – *pulpo* (octopus) is the prize dish. (p53)

Sidrería Vasca Zeraín Sophisticated Basque cooking that shows they're not just obsessed with tapas up north. (p59)

La Cocina de María Luisa The inland cuisine of Castilla y León takes centre stage at this well-regarded Salamanca eatery. (p94)

La Huerta de Tudela Assured cooking from the Navarra region of northeastern Spain. (p58)

Biotza The best in Basque cooking from bite-sized *pintxos* (Basque tapas) to sit-down meals out back. (p94)

Worth a Trip

DiverXo (☎915 70 07 66; diverxo.com; Calle de Padre Damián, 23; mains €70-90, set menus €95-200; ⏱2-3.30pm & 9-10.30pm Tue-Sat, closed three weeks in Aug; Ⓜ Cuzco) in northern Madrid is the city's only three-Michelín-starred restaurant. Chef David Muñoz, something of the *enfant terrible* of Spain's cooking scene, favours what he calls a 'brutal' approach to cooking – his team of chefs appear mid-bite to add surprising new ingredients.

Best
Tapas

LUIS DAVILLA/GETTY IMAGES ©

The art of *ir de tapear* (going out for tapas) is one of Madrid's most enduring and best-loved gastronomic and social traditions (p46) rolled into one. Many of the city's best tapas bars clamour for space in La Latina, but such is the local love of tapas that every Madrid *barrio* has some fabulous options.

Best for Tapas

Estado Puro Madrid's most innovative tapas from the kitchen lab of masterchef Paco Roncero. (p124)

Taberna Matritum Slightly removed from the main La Latina tapas zone, but worth the slight detour. (p44)

Juana La Loca Wins our vote for Madrid's best *tortilla de patatas* (Spanish omelette). (p45)

Txirimiri Fantastic *tortilla de patatas* and so much more, with a Basque theme for much of what's on offer. (p45)

Casa Alberto Tapas like *jamón* (ham) and *croquetas* (croquettes) as they used to be in a traditional setting. (p57)

Ramiro's Tapas Wine Bar One of the trendiest tapas bars in the city, with that traditional-fusion thing down pat. (p58)

Casa Revuelta A Madrid institution for the city's best cod bites, as well as tripe and bacon bits. (p32)

Bocaito Classic Andalucian tapas, and bar staff who keep things loud and ticking over. (p108)

Mercado de San Miguel Fresh produce market meets delicatessen with some of Madrid's most desirable tapas. (p32)

Best
Cafes

Madrid's thriving cafe culture dates back to the early to mid-20th century, when old-style coffee-houses formed the centrepiece of the country's intellectual life. Many have been lost to time, but some outstanding examples remain and their clientele long ago broadened to encompass an entire cross-section of modern Madrid society. To these age-old institutions have been added newer places that nonetheless serve a similar purpose, at once capturing the purpose of the Madrid-cafe-as-meeting-place and evoking the nostalgia of the past. Most of the cafes covered here are primarily places to take a coffee at any hour of the day or early evening, and we recommend them as such. But this being Spain, the majority stays open well beyond midnight. They all serve alcohol if you're in need of something a little stronger.

MARK READ/LONELY PLANET ©

Best Old Literary Cafes

Café-Restaurante El Espejo Another of the grand old dames of Madrid high society, this storied cafe retains its original decor. (p110)

Gran Café de Gijón The third in a triumvirate of cafes that rank among Europe's best. (p110)

Cafe de Oriente Fabulous palace views and a stately Central European feel. (p34)

Best Meeting Places

Café Manuela Old-world decoration and the lively hum of modern Madrid – a perfect mix. (p110)

Café del Real Cool and intimate urban space in the heart of the city. (p34)

Lolina Vintage Café One of Malasaña's coolest retro cafes, with coffee, cocktails and a mixed Malasaña crowd. (p103)

Best
Shopping

Madrid is a great place to shop, and shopping in the Spanish capital often involves debunking a few stereotypes. Fashionistas will discover a whole new world of designers and discover in the process that there's so much more to Spanish fashion than Zara and Mango. The buzz surrounding Spanish food and drink is not restricted to the city's restaurants and tapas bars, as there are some fine purveyors of gourmet foods where you can shop for goodies to carry back home. And then there are the antiques and quality souvenirs that more than compensate for the tacky flamenco dresses and bull T-shirts that can assail visitors at every turn.

Spanish Fashions

Just as Spanish celebrity chefs have taken the world by storm, the world's most prestigious catwalks are clamouring for Spanish designers. The bold colours and eye-catching designs may be relative newcomers on the international stage, but they've been around in Madrid for far longer, with most designers making their names during the creative outpouring of *la movida madrileña* in the 1980s.

Gourmet Foods

Madrid's markets have undergone something of a revolution in recent years, transforming into vibrant spaces where you can eat as well as shop. Added to these are the small specialist stores where the packaging is often as exquisite as the tastes on offer.

Antiques & Souvenirs

You *could* buy your friends back home a bullfighting poster with their names on it. Or you could go for a touch more class and take home a lovely papier mâché figurine, a carefully crafted ceramic bowl or a hand-painted Spanish fan.

CHRIS MELLOR/GETTY IMAGES ©

Best for Spanish Fashions

Agatha Ruiz de la Prada The icon of a generation, Agatha's outrageous colours make her the Pedro Almodóvar of Spanish fashion. (p89)

Camper Only Spanish designers could make a world fashion superstar out of bowling-shoe chic. (p88)

Manolo Blahnik The world-famous maker of designer shoes for celebrities from all corners of the globe. (p89)

Gallery Stunning Salamanca space, with uber-cool accessories a trademark. (p96)

Above: Mantequería Bravo (p97)

Best for Gourmet Foods

Mercado de San Miguel Cured meats all vacuum-sealed and ready to take home is just one of the things this remodelled market does so well. (p32)

Bombonerías Santa Old-style and near-perfect chocolates gift-wrapped like works of art. (p89)

Oriol Balaguer One of Spain's most celebrated pastry chefs is also a chocolatier par excellence. (p89)

Mantequería Bravo The best old-style Spanish deli in Madrid. (p97)

Best for Antiques & Souvenirs

El Arco Artesanía Designer souvenirs from papier mâché to ceramics and scarves right on Plaza Mayor. (p36)

Antigua Casa Talavera Ceramics and tileworks with an individual touch from family potters across the Spanish interior. (p36)

Casa Hernanz Rope-soled *alpargatas* (espadrilles) are the perfect souvenir of the Spanish summer. (p36)

Maty Flamenco dresses and shoes that have the stamp of authenticity. (p37)

Casa Postal Old postcards and posters dominate this hoary old Aladdin's Cave. (p113)

Botería Julio Rodríguez Old Spanish wineskins as they used to be. (p49)

Best **Art**

Madrid is one of the great art capitals of the world. The city's astonishing collection of art museums is the legacy of self-aggrandising Spanish royals of centuries past who courted the great painters of the day and built up peerless collections of masterpieces from all across Europe.

The Golden Mile

Few streets on the planet have the artistic pedigree of the Paseo del Prado. Arrayed along (or just set back from) its shores are three of the world's best art galleries, known locally as the Prado, Thyssen and Reina Sofía. Together their collections form a catalogue of breathtaking breadth and richness, spanning the generations of Spanish masters from Goya to Picasso, with all the major European masters thrown in for good measure.

Beyond the Paseo del Prado

In the rush to Madrid's big three art museums, visitors too often neglect (or fail to realise that they're alongside) other galleries that would be major attractions in any other city. These include one of the few places where Goya's paintings remain in their original setting; an art college where all the Spanish greats studied; and a gallery devoted entirely to Joaquín Sorolla, one of Spain's most admired painters but little known beyond Spanish shores. And from the Prado and Reina Sofía to the Caixa Forum and Museo Sorolla, the buildings in which these collections hang rank among Madrid's most artistic architectural forms.

Best for Spanish Masters

Museo del Prado Come for Goya and Velázquez, but stay all day for a journey through the richest centuries of European art. A worthy rival to the Louvre – it's that good. (p66)

Real Academia de Bellas Artes de San Fernando Picasso and Dalí studied here, and there are works by Goya, Picasso, Velázquez and Zurbarán to name just some of the household names you'll find here. (p55)

Ermita de San Antonio de la Florida Extraordinary frescoes painted by Goya in 1798 remain *in situ* in this unassuming little hermitage – one of Madrid's most underrated attractions. (p114)

Left: Museo del Prado (p66); Above: San Lorenzo de El Escorial (p119)

Best for Contemporary Art

Centro de Arte Reina Sofía Picasso's *Guernica* and the artist's preparatory sketches steal the show, but there's also Salvador Dalí, Joan Miró and the leading artists of 20th-century Spain. (p72)

Caixa Forum Avant-garde architecture provides the stage for a rich and revolving round of temporary exhibitions across a range of genres that include photography, painting and installation art. (p83)

Best of the Rest

Museo Thyssen-Bornemisza Private collection that encompasses the great names of European art, beginning in medieval times and reaching a crescendo with Jackson Pollock and Mark Rothko. (p76)

Museo Sorolla Valencian artist whose paintings (and former home that houses them) capture the essence of the Mediterranean. (p117)

Museo Lázaro Galdiano Another stellar private collection with Goya, El Greco and Constable in a fine old Salamanca mansion. (p86)

San Lorenzo de El Escorial El Greco and so many other minor masters add art gallery to this palace-monastery complex's myriad charms. (p119)

Worth a Trip

Northwest of Plaza de España, the **Museo de Cerralbo** (☎91 547 36 46; en.museocerralbo.mcu.es; Calle de Ventura Rodríguez 17; adult/concession €3/free, free Sun, 2-3pm Sat, 5-8pm Thu; ⏱9.30am-3pm Tue, Wed, Fri & Sat, 9.30am-3pm & 5-8pm Thu, 10am-3pm Sun; Ⓜ Ventura Rodríguez) is a noble old mansion jammed with everything from Asian pieces to religious paintings and clocks. Amid it all are magnificent artworks by Zurbarán, Ribera, Van Dyck and El Greco.

Best Green Spaces

Once you escape the very heart of downtown Madrid, the city begins to breathe. The most obvious choice for an escape into the greenery is the Parque del Buen Retiro, one of Europe's loveliest parks and monumental gardens, but there are plenty of other options. The footpaths running down the middle of the Paseo del Prado are gloriously shady, presided over by trees planted in the 18th century, and lined on one side by the Real Jardín Botánico, Madrid's botanical gardens. And west of the centre, the lovely Parque del Oeste drops down the hill from the *barrio* of Argüelles, Campo de Moro extends out behind the Palacio Real and the Casa de Campo is a vast stand of greenery even further away to the west.

PALERMO SICILY/GETTY IMAGES ©

Best Beyond the Centre

Casa de Campo A vast parkland west of downtown Madrid, with restaurants, a cable car, lake, zoo and fun park.

Campo del Moro The Retiro's rival for the title of Madrid's loveliest park – it's hidden down the hill behind the royal palace. (Map p28, A4)

Best Parks

Parque del Buen Retiro Madrid's loveliest and largest stand of green, dotted with monuments and filled with empty lawns. (p80)

Jardines de Sabatini Manicured gardens in the shadow of the Palacio Real, with fountains and maze-like hedges. (p27)

Plaza de Olavide One of Madrid's greenest squares, with shaded bars around the perimeter. (p117)

Real Jardín Botánico Pathways wind between vast stands of plants, exotic and otherwise, a few steps from the Museo del Prado in the heart of town. (Map p82, B4)

Best
For Kids

Like all major cities, Madrid requires you to plan carefully to make sure that your children enjoy their visit to the city as much as you do. The major art galleries sometimes have activities for children, while most also have printed guides to their collections designed for them. Public playgrounds also inhabit many city squares – ask the tourist office if they know the nearest one – and the Parque del Buen Retiro has a host of child-centric activities on offer. And remember that Madrid is an extremely child-friendly city in the sense that children will be welcome in most bars and all but the most formal restaurants, with waiters usually happy to offer suggestions for meals. An increasing (though still small) number of restaurants have children's menus.

MARK AVELLINO/GETTY IMAGES ©

Parque del Buen Retiro
Playgrounds, vast open spaces, boat rides, bike hire and occasional puppet shows. (p80)

Zoo Aquarium de Madrid (📞 902 345 014; www.zoomadrid.com; Casa de Campo; adult/child €22.95/18.60; ⏰ 10.30am-10pm Sun-Thu, 10.30am-midnight Fri & Sat Jul & Aug, shorter hours Sep-Jun; 🚌 37 from Intercambiador de Príncipe Pío, Ⓜ Casa de Campo) An attractive zoo with a full range of species in Casa de Campo.

Parque de Atracciones (📞 91 463 29 00; www.parquedeatracciones.es; Casa de Campo; adult/child €31.90/24.90; ⏰ noon-midnight Jul & Aug, shorter hours Sep-Jun; Ⓜ Batán) Amusement park with rides for all ages.

Teleférico (📞 91 541 11 18; www.teleferico.com; cnr Paseo del Pintor Rosales & Calle de Marqués de Urquijo; one way/return €4.20/5.90; ⏰ noon-9pm May-Aug, reduced hours Sep-Apr; Ⓜ Argüelles) A trundling cable car that connects the Paseo de Pinto Rosales to Casa de Campo.

Estadio Santiago Bernabéu (📞 91 398 43 00, tickets 902 324 324, tour 91 398 43 70; www.realmadrid.com; Av de Concha Espina 1; tour adult/child €19/13; ⏰ tours 10am-7pm Mon-Sat, 10.30am-6.30pm Sun, except match days; Ⓜ Santiago Bernabéu) Home of Real Madrid and one of the most impressive football stadiums on earth, with tours, a museum, and matches from August to May.

Casa Museo de Ratón Perez (📞 91 522 69 68; www.casamuseoratonperez.com; 1st fl, Calle de Arenal 8; admission €3; ⏰ 5-8pm Mon, 11am-2pm & 5-8pm Tue-Fri, 11am-3pm & 4-8pm Sat; Ⓜ Sol) Guided visits for kids through the home of Spain's version of the tooth fairy.

Best
Bars

Nights in the Spanish capital are the stuff of legend and what Hemingway wrote of the city in the 1930s remains true to this day: 'Nobody goes to bed in Madrid until they have killed the night.' Madrid has more bars than any city in the world, six, in fact, for every 100 inhabitants, and wherever you are in town, there'll be a bar close by.

Pre-Dinner Drinks

If you're unaccustomed to Madrid's late eating hours, the upside is that it allows plenty of time for a pre-dinner drink, an activity that locals have turned into an institution. Of course, they often combine the two – eating and drinking – by starting early with a drink and some tapas. So in addition to the bars we cover in these lists, it's always worth considering those places better known for their food when planning your first step into the night because they're often terrific places to drink as well.

Opening Hours

Madrid's bars range from simple, local watering holes that serve as centres of community life to sophisticated temples to good taste. The former usually open throughout the day, while the latter rarely do so before 8pm. Otherwise, some places may close half an hour earlier or later (especially on Friday and Saturday nights), but 3am operates as a threshold. The hours between midnight and 3am are filled with choices, although we recommend that you take up residence in one of the oh-so-cool cocktail bars.

Best Cocktail Bars

Museo Chicote Madrid's most famous cocktail bar, beloved by celebrities from Hemingway to Sophia Loren. (p108)

Del Diego A quieter venue for A-list *famosos*, with near-perfect (and always creative) cocktails. (p110)

1862 Dry Bar Creative cocktails in sophisticated surrounds down on happening Calle del Pez. (p112)

Rooftop Bars

La Terraza del Urban The height of class on a warm summer's evening. (p60)

The Roof Slick venue high above Plaza de Santa Ana with sky-high admission prices to match. (p53)

Above: Museo Chicote (p108)

Gau&Café Cool and casual bar alongside the Lavapiés rooftops. (p48)

Old Barrio Bars

La Venencia A timeless sherry bar where old barrels abound, close to Plaza de Santa Ana. (p59)

Bodega de la Ardosa Another neighbourhood classic north of the centre. (p117)

Best of the Rest

Café Belén Chilled bar staff, chilled punters and fabulous mojitos. (p110)

Delic Wonderful setting on a medieval square and mojitos of the highest order. (p41)

El Imperfecto Great cocktails and a real Huertas buzz make this one of Madrid's best bars. (p60)

Taberna Tempranillo A great La Latina wine bar along Calle de la Cava Baja, with an entire wall of wine bottles. (p48)

Anticafé Bohemian decor and an alternative slant on life. (p35)

Taberna La Dolores Classy and historic bar in the Paseo del Prado hinterland. (p53)

Worth a Trip

Overlooking one of the most famous football fields on earth, the **Real Café Bernabéu** (91 458 36 67; www.realcafe bernabeu.es; Gate 30, Estadio Santiago Bernabéu, Av de Concha Espina; 9pm-1am; M Santiago Bernabéu) is a trendy cocktail bar with exceptional views and a steady stream of beautiful people among the clientele. It closes two hours before a game and doesn't open until an hour after.

Best
Live Music & Flamenco

MARK READ/GETTY IMAGES ©

Madrid has a happening live-music scene, which owes a lot to the city's role as the cultural capital of the Spanish-speaking world. There's flamenco, world-class jazz and a host of performers you may never have heard of – one of whom may just be Spain's next big thing. For something more edifying, there's opera and *zarzuela* (mix of theatre, music and dance).

Flamenco

Flamenco's roots lie in Andalucía, but the top performers gravitate towards Madrid for live performances; in June, Madrid hosts the prestigious **Suma Flamenca** (www.madrid.org/sumaflamenca) festival. Remember also that most *tablaos* (flamenco venues) offer meals to go with the floorshow. In our experience, the meals are often overpriced, but if you just pay for the show (the admission usually includes a drink), you may not have the best seat in the house. If possible, buy your ticket in person at the venue to get a sense of where you'll be seated.

Jazz

Madrid has some of Europe's best jazz, with at least three fine venues, one of which was voted one of the world's best not so long ago. Groups often play for a whole week, making it easier to get tickets.

Rock Madrid

At the height of *la movida madrilèna*, the crazy outpouring of creativity and hedonism in Madrid in the 1980s, an estimated 300 rock bands were performing in the bars of Malasaña alone. There aren't quite so many these days, but there are still plenty that capture that spirit.

Best Flamenco

Las Tablas A smaller, more intimate venue with consistently high-quality performances. (p35)

Casa Patas One of Madrid's most celebrated flamenco stages, with a respected flamenco school attached. (p48)

Villa Rosa Once appeared in an Almodóvar movie and has recently returned to its flamenco roots. (p62)

Cardamomo A dimly lit bar where the performances rank among Madrid's best. (p53)

Café de Chinitas A fine stage with an elegant setting. (p35)

Best Jazz

Café Central Regularly ranked among the elite of world jazz clubs; all the

Above: Teatro Real (p36)

big names have played beneath the fabulous art deco decor. (p62)

Populart A more earthy (and free) venue; the acts here are often the rivals of Café Central, its more illustrious neighbour up the road. (p53)

Casa Pueblo Free jazz in a knowledgeable, casual bar setting. (p53)

El Junco Jazz Club Live jazz then dancing all night: it's a fine combination. (p112)

Best Rock & the Rest

Sala El Sol One of the legends of 1980s Madrid and still going strong. (p62)

Costello Café & Niteclub A sophisticated venue that feels like a SoHo cocktail bar. (p63)

ContraClub Rock is often part of a diverse mix at this live-music-venue-slash-club. (p49)

Best High Culture

Teatro Real Spain's finest opera performers take to the stage at this acoustically perfect venue. (p36)

Teatro de la Zarzuela Madrid's very own cross between theatre and opera; the theatre also hosts the finest in contemporary dance. (p62)

Worth a Trip

Honky Tonk (📞 91 445 61 91; www.clubhonky.com; Calle de Covarrubias 24; ⏰ 9.30pm-5am Sun-Thu, 9.30pm-6am Fri & Sat; Ⓜ Alonso Martínez) is a great place to see blues or local rock 'n' roll, though many acts have a little country, jazz or R&B thrown into the mix, too. It's a fun vibe in a smallish club that's been around since the heady 1980s and opens 365 days a year.

Best **Clubs**

Madrid nights are long and loud and people here live fully for the moment. Today's encounter can be tomorrow's distant memory, perhaps in part because Madrid's nightclubs (also known as *discotecas*) rival any in the world. The best places are usually the megaclubs with designer decor, designer people and, sometimes, with enough space for numerous dance floors each with their own musical style to suit your mood. Themed nights are all the rage, so it's always worth checking in advance to see what flavour of the night takes your fancy. Although you'll find a nightclub going strong until sunrise in almost every *barrio*, the biggest selection of clubs is to be found downtown.

LONELY PLANET/GETTY IMAGES ©

Almonte Flamenco tunes and a formidable cast of amateur flamenco wannabes make for an alternative slant to the night. (p95)

Serrano 41 Keep your eyes peeled for the Real Madrid set; it has a tough door policy, as you'd expect. (p96)

Opening Hours & Admission

Most nightclubs don't open until around midnight, don't really get going until after 1am, and some won't even bat an eyelid until 3am, when the bars elsewhere have closed. Admission prices vary widely, but the standard admission costs around €12. Even those that let you in for free will play catch-up with hefty drinks prices, so don't plan your night around looking for the cheapest ticket.

Teatro Joy Eslava Enduringly popular converted theatre with great music, live acts and a fun crowd. (p35)

Kapital Madrid's megaclub of longest standing with seven floors and something for everyone. (p83)

Ya'sta Thirty years on, this Malasaña epic just keeps rolling on into the night. (p112)

Charada Former brothel where you can wave your hands in the air like you just don't care. (p35)

Best
Gay & Lesbian

JAVIER SORIANO/GETTY IMAGES ©

It's a great time to be gay in Madrid. Under laws passed by the Spanish Congress in 2005, same-sex marriages now enjoy the same legal protection as those between heterosexual partners. Opinion polls at the time showed that the reforms were supported by more than two-thirds of Spaniards. And Madrid has always been one of Europe's most gay-friendly cities, anyway. The city's gay community is credited with reinvigorating the once down-at-heel inner-city *barrio* of Chueca, where Madrid didn't just come out of the closet, but ripped the doors off in the process. Today the *barrio* is one of Madrid's most vibrant and it's very much the heart and soul of gay Madrid. Cafes, bars and nightclubs clearly oriented to a gay clientele abound, and book, video and adult-toy shops aimed at gay people continue to spring up in and around Chueca, as do gay-friendly hostels. But there's nothing ghetto-like about Chueca. Its extravagantly gay and lesbian personality is anything but exclusive, and the crowd is almost always mixed gay–straight. As gay and lesbian residents like to say, Chueca isn't gay-friendly, it's hetero-friendly.

Café Acuarela A huge, nude male statue guards the doorway at this agreeable, dimly lit salon centrepiece of gay Madrid. (p110)

Why Not? Almost anything goes at this reliably intimate nightclub where gay and straight couples merge seamlessly. (p111)

Black & White Few venues have the history of this place; it's been here since Chueca turned gay. Expect cabaret and just about anything else. (p112)

Diurno Cafe-style ambience and an enduring if understated social hub for Chueca's gay community. (p111)

Best
For Free

Best Always-Free Places

Ermita de San Antonio de la Florida Goya's frescoes are free, just where he painted them. (p114)

Caixa Forum Admire the architecture before deciding whether to pay for one of the exhibitions. (p83)

El Rastro The Sunday-morning flea market is one of Madrid's premier attractions. (p40)

Parque del Buen Retiro One of Europe's grand-est, most beautiful city parks. (p136)

Estación de Chamberí Take a journey under-ground to Madrid's ghost metro station. (p117)

Templo de Debod Ma-drid's very own Egyptian temple doesn't cost a cent, nor does the lovely parkland that surrounds it. (p115)

Museo al Aire Libre Outdoor sculptures by some of Spain's best-known artists. (p92)

Plaza de Toros & Museo Taurino Visits to the bullring and its museum, though you pay for tours and bullfights. (p98)

Museo de Historia Free journey through Madrid's past, complete with a Goya. (p106)

Best Sometimes-Free Places

Museo del Prado Free 6pm to 8pm Monday to Saturday, and 5pm to 7pm Sunday. (p66)

Museo Thyssen-Bornemisza Free Monday. (p76)

Centro de Arte Reina Sofía Free 1.30pm to 7pm Sunday, and 7pm to 9pm Monday and Wednesday to Saturday. (p72)

Real Academia de Bellas Artes de San Fernando Free Wednesday. (p55)

Basílica de San Fran-cisco El Grande Free during mass times. (p44)

JOHN BORTHWICK/GETTY IMAGES ©

☑ Top Tip

▶ South of the centre and next to the revamped Madrid riverfront, **Matadero Madrid** (☎91 252 52 53; www.mataderomadrid.com; Paseo de la Chopera 14; admission free; Ⓜ Le-gazpi) is a stunning contemporary-arts centre that occupies the converted buildings of an old livestock market and slaughterhouse. It hosts cutting-edge drama, musical and dance performanc-es, and exhibitions.

Survival Guide

Survival Guide

Before You Go

When to Go

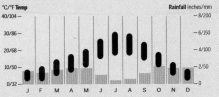

°C/°F Temp
40/104 —
30/86 —
20/68 —
10/50 —
0/32 —

Rainfall Inches/mm
— 8/200
— 6/150
— 4/100
— 2/50
— 0

J F M A M J J A S O N D

➡ **Summer (Jun–Aug)**
Can be fiercely hot; many locals desert the city; in August, many restaurants close and sights operate on reduced hours.

➡ **Autumn (Sep–Nov)**
Nice time to visit with mild temperatures; warmish in September, cool in November.

➡ **Winter (Dec–Feb)**
Can be bitterly cold; snow possible but often clear skies; Christmas is a festive time in the city; flamenco festival in February.

➡ **Spring (Mar–May)**
Mild temperatures; Semana Santa (Easter) and May festivals.

Book Your Stay

➡ In Madrid, a *habitación doble* (double room) usually indicates a room with two single beds; cuddly couples should request a *cama de matrimonio* (literally, a marriage bed).

➡ Royal Madrid and anywhere around Sol, La Latina and Huertas puts you within walking distance of most sights and plenty of restaurants, but it can be noisy.

➡ Salamanca and the Paseo del Prado tend to be more upmarket and generally quieter.

➡ Malasaña and Chueca are a little removed from the major sights (it's all relative – you're still walking distance away), but they offer fascinating insights into local life.

➡ Be wary of high season (*temporada alta*), which in Madrid can depend more on trade fairs than the weather.

Useful Websites

→ **Lonely Planet** (www.lonelyplanet.com) Author recommendations and online booking.

→ **Apartasol** (www.apartasol.com) Apartments around the centre.

→ **EsMadrid** (www.esmadrid.com/en/where-to-stay) Tourist office overview of accommodation.

Best Budget

→ **Madrid City Rooms** (www.madridcityrooms.com) Outstanding service and excellent rooms in the centre.

→ **Lapepa Chic B&B** (http://lapepa-bnb.com) Fabulous budget B&B with attention to detail.

→ **Hostal Main Street Madrid** (www.mainstreetmadrid.com) Central and very cool *hostal* (budget hotel).

→ **Flat 5 Madrid** (www.flat5madrid.com) One of Madrid's best deals away from the tourist hordes.

→ **Hostal Madrid** (www.hostal-madrid.info) Recently renovated rooms and friendly service downtown.

Best Midrange

→ **Hostal Central Palace Madrid** (http://central

palacemadrid.com) Some of the best views in Madrid, whatever the price.

→ **Posada del León de Oro** (www.posadadelleondeoro.com) La Latina at its most atmospheric.

→ **Catalonia Las Cortes** (www.hoteles-catalonia.es) Great rooms, service and Huertas location.

→ **NH Collection Palacio de Tepa** (www.nh-collection.com) Palace on the outside, stylish rooms within.

→ **Praktik Metropol** (www.hotelpraktikmetropol.com) Great views, cool rooms and fun atmosphere.

Best Top End

→ **Hotel Orfila** (www.hotelorfila.com) Unquestionable luxury with service to match.

→ **Hotel Ritz** (www.ritzmadrid.com) Quite simply one of Europe's grandest hotels.

→ **Villa Magna** (www.villamagna.es) Refined Salamanca address for the well-heeled.

→ **Westin Palace** (www.westinpalacemadrid.com) Near faultless five-star address close to Paseo del Prado.

→ **Hotel Urban** (www.derbyhotels.com) Swish downtown temple to modern luxury.

Arriving in Madrid

From Aeropuerto de Barajas

→ **Metro** (one way €4.50; 6.05am to 1.30am; 15 to 25 minutes; line 8) Runs to the Nuevos Ministerios transport interchange, which connects with lines 10 and 6. Buy tickets at the airport station.

→ **Bus** The Exprés Aeropuerto (Airport Express; www.emtmadrid.es; €5; 40 minutes; 24 hour) runs between Puerta de Atocha train station and the airport. From 11.30pm until 6am, departures are from the Plaza de Cibeles, not the train station.

→ **Taxi** A taxi to the centre (around 30 minutes, depending on traffic) costs a fixed €30.

→ **Minibus** Aero City (www.aerocity.com; 24 hour) is a private minibus service that takes you door-to-door between hotels and the airport. Prices vary according to the number of people but are generally cheaper than taxis.

From Estación de Atocha

➡ **Metro** (one-way/10-trip ticket €1.50/12.20; 6am to 1.30am; line 1) From Atocha Renfe station to Sol (10 to 15 minutes) with connections elsewhere via lines 2 and 3. Buy tickets from machines at the station.

➡ **Taxi** A taxi to the centre (around 10 minutes, depending on traffic) costs €5 to €7.50, plus a €3 train-station supplement.

From Estación de Chamartín

➡ **Metro** (one-way/10-trip ticket €1.50/12.20; 6am-1am; lines 1 and 10) From Chamartín station to Sol (15 to 20 minutes) with connections elsewhere via lines 2 and 3. Buy tickets from machines at the station.

➡ **Taxi** A taxi to the centre (around 15 minutes, depending on traffic) costs around €10, plus a €3 train-station supplement.

☑ **Top Tip** For the best way to get to your accommodation, see p17.

Getting Around

Metro

☑ **Best for...** Madrid's metro is almost always the best choice, with an extensive network of lines and stations throughout the city.

➡ **Metro de Madrid** (www. metromadrid.es) Runs a metro system with 12 colour-coded lines.

➡ Single tickets, good for one journey, cost €1.50 and can be bought at metro stations and news kiosks, but it's almost

always better to buy the 10-trip ticket for €12.20.

➡ The metro operates from 6.05am to 1.30am.

Bus

☑ **Best for...** Night trips when the metro shuts down, travellers who find metro stairs are impassable (eg people with prams, travellers with disabilities) and seeing a little of Madrid above ground as you get around.

➡ **EMT buses** (www. emtmadrid.es) Travel along most city routes regularly between about 6.30am and 11.30pm.

➡ Twenty-six night-bus búhos (owls) routes operate from 11.45pm to 5.30am, with all routes originating in Plaza de la Cibeles.

➡ Fares for day and night trips are the same: €1.50 for a single trip, €12.20 for a 10-trip Metrobús ticket. Single-trip tickets can be purchased on board.

Cercanías

☑ **Best for...** Getting to San Lorenzo de El Escorial, or a quick north–south trip between Chamartín and Atocha train stations (with stops at Nuevos Ministerios and Sol).

Tickets & Passes

Ten-trip Metrobús tickets will save you time and money and are sold in machines at all metro stations, as well as most newspaper kiosks and *estancos* (tobacconists). A 10-trip ticket (€12.20) is valid on the metro and EMT buses. An *Abono Transporte Turístico* (Tourist Ticket; per 1/2/7 days €8.40/14.20/35.40) is also available.

- The short-range *cercanías* trains operated by **Renfe** (www.renfe.es/cercanias/madrid) go places that the metro doesn't.
- Tickets range between €1.70 and €8.70 depending on how far you're travelling.

Taxi

☑ **Best for...** Quick trips across town outside peak hours

- Taxis are reasonably priced and charges are posted on the inside of passenger-side windows. The trip from Sol to the Museo del Prado costs about €5.
- You can call a taxi at **Tele-Taxi** (91 371 21 31; www.tele-taxi.es) and **Radio-Teléfono Taxi** (91 547 82 00; www.radiotelefono-taxi.com) or flag one down in the street.

Essential Information

Business Hours

- **Banks** 8.30am to 2pm Monday to Friday; some also open 4pm to 7pm Thursday.
- **Central Post Offices** 8.30am to 9.30pm Monday to Friday, 8.30am to 2pm Saturday.
- **Restaurants** Lunch 1pm to 4pm, dinner 8.30pm to midnight.
- **Shops** 10am to 2pm and 4.30pm to 7.30pm or 5pm to 8pm.

Discount Cards

- Student cards offer discounts of up to 50% at many sights.
- If you're over 65, you may be eligible for an admission discount to some attractions, although such discounts are often only available for EU citizens and residents.
- If you intend to do some intensive sightseeing and travelling on public transport, it might be worth looking at the **Madrid Card** (91 360 47 72; www.madridcard.com; 1/2/3/5 days adult €47/60/67/77, child aged 6-12 €34/42/44/47). It includes free entry to more than 40 museums in and around Madrid.
- If you plan to visit the Museo del Prado, Museo Thyssen-Bornemisza and Centro de Arte Reina Sofía while in Madrid, the Paseo del Arte ticket covers them all in a combined ticket for €25.60; buying separate tickets would cost €32.

Electricity

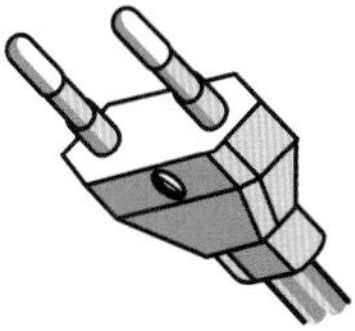

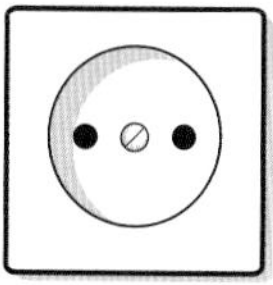

220V/230V/50Hz

Emergency

- **Servicio de Atención al Turista Extranjero** (Foreign Tourist Assistance Service; 91 548 80 08, 91 548 85 37; www.esmadrid.com/informacion-turistica/sate; Calle de Leganitos 19; 9am-midnight; M Plaza de España, Santo Domingo) Specially trained officers can assist with contacting your embassy or your family, as well as cancelling credit cards.
- **Ambulance** (061)

→ **EU standard emergency number** (☎112)

→ **Fire Brigade** (Bomberos; ☎080)

→ **Policía Nacional** (☎091)

Money

→ **Currency** Euro (€)

→ **ATMs** Widely available; usually a charge on ATM cash withdrawals abroad.

→ **Cash** Banks and building societies offer the best rates; take your passport.

→ **Credit cards** Accepted in most hotels, restaurants and shops; may need to show passport or other photo ID.

Money-Saving Tips

→ Look out for free entry at sights (see p114).

→ Order the *menú del día* for lunch in restaurants.

→ Buy discount cards (see p149).

→ Buy 10-trip travel cards to get around the city (see p148).

→ **Tipping** Small change in restaurants, round up to the nearest euro in taxis.

Public Holidays

Many shops are closed and many attractions operate on reduced hours on the following dates:

Año Nuevo (New Year's Day) 1 January

Reyes (Epiphany or Three Kings' Day) 6 January

Jueves Santo (Holy Thursday) March/April

Viernes Santo (Good Friday) March/April

Fiesta del Trabajo (Labour Day) 1 May

Fiesta de la Comunidad de Madrid 2 May

Fiestas de San Isidro Labrador 15 May

La Asunción (Feast of the Assumption) 15 August

Día de la Hispanidad (Spanish National Day) 12 October

Día de Todos los Santos (All Saints' Day) 1 November

Día de la Virgen de la Almudena 9 November

Día de la Constitución (Constitution Day) 6 December

La Inmaculada Concepción (Feast of the Immaculate Conception) 8 December

Navidad (Christmas) 25 December

Safe Travel

Petty crime and theft, with tourists as the prey of choice, can be a problem in Madrid, although most visitors encounter few problems. Take particular care on the metro, at the El Rastro Sunday morning flea market, and around attractions popular with tourists (such as the Museo del Prado).

Telephone

Mobile Phones

→ Spanish mobile phones have nine digits and begin with a '6'.

→ Local SIM cards are widely available and can be used in European and Australian mobile phones. Other phones may need to be set to roaming.

Phone Codes

→ **International access code** (☎00)

→ **Spain country code** (☎34)

Useful Numbers

➡ **International directory inquiries** (☎11825)

➡ **International operator and reverse charges (collect)** Europe (☎1008); rest of world (☎1005)

Toilets

Public toilets are almost nonexistent in Madrid, and it's not really the done thing to go into a bar or cafe solely to use the toilet; ordering a quick coffee is a small price to pay.

Tourist Information

➡ **Centro de Turismo de Madrid** (Map p28; ☎010, 91 454 44 10; www.esmadrid.com; Plaza Mayor 27; ☻9.30am-8.30pm; ⓂSol) Madrid government's Centro de Turismo is terrific.

➡ **Centro de Turismo Colón** (www.esmadrid.com; Plaza de Colón 1; ☻9.30am-8.30pm; ⓂColón) A smaller tourist office accessible via the underground stairs on the corner of Calle de Goya and Paseo de la Castellana.

➡ **Punto de Información Turística de Cibeles** (www.esmadrid.com; Plaza de la Cibeles; ☻9.30am-8.30pm; ⓂBanco de España)

➡ **Punto de Información Turística CentroCentro** (www.esmadrid.com; Plaza de la Cibeles 1; ☻10am-8pm Tue-Sun; ⓂBanco de España)

➡ **Punto de Información Turística del Paseo del Arte** (www.esmadrid.com; cnr Calle de Santa Isabel & Plaza del Emperador Carlos V; ☻9.30am-8.30pm; ⓂAtocha)

➡ **Punto de Información Turística Adolfo Suárez Madrid-Barajas T2** (www.esmadrid.com; between Salas 5 & 6; ☻9am-8pm)

➡ **Punto de Información Turística Adolfo Suárez Madrid-Barajas T4** (www.esmadrid.com; Salas 10 & 11; ☻9am-8pm)

Travellers with Disabilities

➡ Go to the section of the Madrid tourist office website known as **Accessible Madrid** (www.esmadrid.com/en/madridaccesible), where you can download a pdf of their excellent, 421-page *Guia de Turismo Accesible* in English or Spanish. It has an exhaustive list of the city's attractions and transport and a detailed assessment of their accessibility, as well as a list of accessible restaurants.

Dos & Don'ts

➡ Greet people with the full '*Hola, buenos días*' (morning) or '*Hola, buenas tardes*' (afternoon).

➡ In a social setting, it is customary to greet people with a kiss on each cheek, although two men will only do this if close friends.

➡ For hotels and *hostales*, go to 'Alojamientos Accesibles' to download the website's excellent *Guia de Alojamiento Accesible*.

➡ The tourist office's program of guided tours includes tours for blind, deaf and wheelchair-bound travellers, as well as travellers with an intellectual disability.

Visas

➡ Citizens or residents of EU and Schengen countries: no visa required.

➡ Citizens or residents of Australia, Canada, Israel, Japan, NZ and the USA: no visa required for tourist visits of up to 90 days every six months.

➡ Other countries: check with a Spanish embassy or consulate.

Language

Spanish *(español)* – often referred to
as *castellano* (Castilian) to distinguish
it from other languages spoken in
Spain – is the language of Madrid.
While you'll find an increasing number of *madrileños* who speak some
English, especially younger people and
hotel and restaurant employees, don't
count on it. Travellers who learn a
little Spanish will be amply rewarded
as Spaniards appreciate the effort, no
matter how basic your understanding
of the language.

Most Spanish sounds are pronounced
the same as their English counterparts.
Just read our pronunciation guides
as if they were English and you'll be
understood. Note that 'm/f' indicates
masculine and feminine forms.

To enhance your trip with a phrase-
book, visit **lonelyplanet.com**. Lonely
Planet iPhone phrasebooks are available through the Apple App store.

Basics

Hello.
Hola.   o·la

Goodbye.
Adiós.   a·dyos

How are you?
¿Qué tal?   ke tal

Fine, thanks.
Bien, gracias.   byen gra·thyas

Please.
Por favor.   por fa·vor

Thank you.
Gracias.   gra·thyas

Excuse me.
Perdón.   per·don

Sorry.
Lo siento.   lo syen·to

Yes./No.
Sí./No.   see/no

Do you speak (English)?
¿Habla (inglés)?   a·bla (een·gles)

I (don't) understand.
Yo (no) entiendo.   yo (no) en·tyen·do

What's your name?
¿Cómo se   ko·mo se
llama?   lya·ma

My name is ...
Me llamo ...   me lya·mo ...

Eating & Drinking

Can I see the menu, please?
¿Puedo ver el   pwe·do ver el
menu, por favor?   me·noo por fa·vor

I'm a vegetarian. (m/f)
Soy   soy
vegetariano/a.   ve·khe·ta·rya·no/a

Cheers!
¡Salud!   sa·loo

That was delicious!
¡Estaba   es·ta·ba
buenísimo!   bwe·nee·see·mo

The bill, please.
La cuenta,   la kwen·ta
por favor.   por fa·vor

I'd like ...
Quisiera ...   kee·sye·ra ...

a coffee	*un café*	oon ka·fe
a table for two	*una mesa para dos*	oo·na me·sa pa·ra dos
a wine	*un vino*	oon vee·no
two beers	*dos cervezas*	dos ther·ve·thas

Shopping

I'd like to buy ...
Quisiera   kee·*sye*·ra
comprar ...   kom·*prar ...*

Can I look at it?
¿Puedo verlo?   *pwe*·do ver·lo

How much is it?
¿Cuánto cuesta?   *kwan*·to *kwes*·ta

That's very expensive.
Es muy caro.   es mooy *ka*·ro

Can you lower the price?
¿Podría bajar   po·*dree*·a ba·*khar*
un poco   oon *po*·ko
el precio?   el *pre*·thyo

Emergencies

Help!
Socorro!   so·*ko*·ro

Call a doctor!
Llame a   *lya*·me a oon
un médico!   *me*·dee·ko

Call the police!
Llame a   *lya*·me a
la policía!   la po·lee·*thee*·a

I'm lost. (m/f)
Estoy perdido/a.   es·*toy* per·*dee*·do/a

I'm ill. (m/f)
Estoy enfermo/a.   es·*toy* en·*fer*·mo/a

Where are the toilets?
¿Dónde están   *don*·de es·*tan*
los baños?   los *ba*·nyos

Time & Numbers

What time is it?
¿Qué hora es?   ke *o*·ra es

It's (10) o'clock.
Son (las diez).   son (las dyeth)

morning	*mañana*	ma·*nya*·na
afternoon	*tarde*	*tar*·de
evening	*noche*	*no*·che

yesterday	*ayer*	a·*yer*
today	*hoy*	oy
tomorrow	*mañana*	ma·*nya*·na

1	*uno*	*oo*·no
2	*dos*	dos
3	*tres*	tres
4	*cuatro*	*kwa*·tro
5	*cinco*	*theen*·ko
6	*seis*	seys
7	*siete*	*sye*·te
8	*ocho*	*o*·cho
9	*nueve*	*nwe*·ve
10	*diez*	dyeth

Transport & Directions

Where's ...?
¿Dónde está ...?   *don*·de es·*ta ...*

Where's the station?
¿Dónde está   *don*·de es·*ta*
la estación?   la es·ta·*thyon*

What's the address?
¿Cuál es la   kwal es la
dirección?   dee·rek·*thyon*

Can you show me (on the map)?
¿Me lo puede   me lo *pwe*·de
indicar   een·dee·*kar*
(en el mapa)?   (en el *ma*·pa)

I want to go to ...
Quisiera ir a ...   kee·*sye*·ra eer a ...

What time does it arrive/leave?
¿A qué hora   a ke *o*·ra
llega/sale?   *lye*·ga/*sa*·le

Please tell me when we get to ...
¿Puede avisarme   *pwe*·de a·vee·*sar*·me
cuando lleguemos   *kwan*·do lye·*ge*·mos
a ...?   a ...

I want to get off here.
Quiero bajarme   *kye*·ro ba·*khar*·me
aquí.   a·*kee*

Behind the Scenes

Send Us Your Feedback

We love to hear from travellers – your comments help make our books better. We read every word, and we guarantee that your feedback goes straight to the authors. Visit **lonelyplanet.com/contact** to submit your updates and suggestions.

Note: We may edit, reproduce and incorporate your comments in Lonely Planet products such as guidebooks, websites and digital products, so let us know if you don't want your comments reproduced or your name acknowledged. For a copy of our privacy policy visit lonelyplanet.com/privacy.

Anthony's Thanks

Special thanks once again to Itziar Herrán, who brought both wisdom and an eye for detail to her contributions to this book. Thanks also to Marina and Alberto for their unwavering hospitality; to Jo Cooke and Lorna Parkes and Lonely Planet's fine team of editors. And to Marina, Carlota and Valentina – you are everything that is good about this wonderful country.

Acknowledgments

Cover photograph: Palacio Real, Madrid, Paolo Giocoso/4Corners

Photograph on pp4–5: Plaza Mayor, Dragos Cosmin Photos/Getty

This Book

This 4th edition of *Pocket Madrid* was written by Anthony Ham, who also wrote the previous three editions. This guidebook was produced by the following:

Destination Editors Joanna Cooke, Lorna Parkes

Product Editor Martine Power **Coordinating Editor** Simon Williamson **Senior Cartographer** Anthony Phelan **Book Designer** Mazzy Prinsep **Assisting Editors** Sarah Billington, Melanie Dankel, Catherine Naghten, Susan Paterson **Cartographers** Mark Griffiths, Gabriel Lindquist

Cover Researcher Campbell McKenzie **Thanks to** Imogen Bannister, Sasha Baskett, Chris and Victoria Booth, Ryan Evans, Andi Jones, Ute Kolbeck, Derek Manson-Smith, Claire Naylor, Karyn Noble, Diana Saengkham, Ellie Simpson, Angela Tinson, Jennifer van Putten, Tony Wheeler

Index

See also separate subindexes for:

⊗ **Eating p157**

🍸 **Drinking p157**

✪ Entertainment p158

🔒 **Shopping p158**

Sights 000
Map Pages **000**

Our Writer

Anthony Ham

In 2001, Anthony (www.anthonyham.com) fell in love with Madrid on his first visit to the city. Less than a year later, he arrived on a one-way ticket, with not a word of Spanish and not knowing a single person. After 10 years living in the city, he recently returned to Australia with his Spanish-born family, but he still adores his adopted country as much as the first day he arrived. When he's not writing for Lonely Planet, Anthony writes about and photographs Spain, Scandinavia, the Middle East, Australia and Africa for newspapers and magazines around the world.

Published by Lonely Planet Publications Pty Ltd
ABN 36 005 607 983
4th edition – Jan 2016
ISBN 978 1 74321 563 0
© Lonely Planet 2016 Photographs © as indicated 2016
10 9 8 7 6 5 4 3 2 1
Printed in China